The Handbook of Soccer

The Handbook of Soccer

A Complete Guide to Football,
the World Game

DON HOWE
AND
BRIAN SCOVELL

PELHAM BOOKS

PELHAM BOOKS
Published by the Penguin Group
27 Wrights Lane, London W8 5TZ, England
Viking Penguin Inc., 40 West 23rd Street, New York,
New York 10010, USA
Penguin Books Australia Ltd, Ringwood, Victoria,
Australia
Penguin Books Canada Ltd, 2801 John Street,
Markham, Ontario, Canada L3R 1B4
Penguin Books (NZ) Ltd, 182–190 Wairau Road,
Auckland 10, New Zealand

Penguin Books Ltd, Registered Offices:
Harmondsworth, Middlesex, England

First published 1988

Printed and bound in Portugal by Printer Portuguesa

Typeset by Cambrian Typesetters, Frimley, Surrey

British Library Cataloguing in Publication Data

Howe, Don
  The handbook of soccer: a complete guide
to football, the world game.
1. Soccer
I. Title II. Scovell, Brian
796.334 GV943
ISBN 0–7207–1792–2

Acknowledgements

All the photographs are by Bob Thomas Sports Photo-
graphy. The diagrams are by David J. Charles of the
Kirkham Studios, and the line drawings are by
Raymond Turvey.
Designed by Penny Mills.

Contents

Foreword

by Bryan Robson, Captain of England

I have always thought that football needs a book which embraces every aspect of the game, and I believe Don Howe's book comes close to achieving it.

I have a lot of respect for Don as a coach. Our association goes back fourteen years when he signed me as a sixteen-year-old for West Bromwich Albion. He was then the manager at the Hawthorns.

John Trewick, now with Oxford, and I were schoolboy trialists from the North East. We shared an ambition to become international footballers. Don helped me bring about that dream. One of the points he stressed to us from the beginning was that enthusiasm and determination were just as important as ability. He taught us that there is no easy route to the top.

If a young boy wants to follow the path I have been privileged to follow, I recommend that he reads *The Handbook of Soccer*. It is a footballing education, full of good sense and sound advice.

September 1987,
Old Trafford

I

Approach To The Game

Key to Diagrams

Each numbered triangle denotes a player (see below) and the way in which the triangle is facing indicates the direction of play. Different coloured triangles are used to distinguish different teams.

⚠1 : Goalkeeper

⚠2 : Right-back (full-back)

⚠3 : Left-back (full-back)

⚠4 : Right midfield

⚠5 : Right centre-back

⚠6 : Left centre-back

⚠7 : Outside-right (winger)

⚠8 : Left midfield

⚠9 : Centre-forward right (striker)

⚠10 : Centre-forward left (striker)

⚠11 : Outside left (winger)

⚠s : Sweeper

⚠c : Coach

The ball is sometimes indicated with a small black circle: ●

————————▶ : The path of the ball

∿∿∿∿▶ : A player dribbling with the ball

– – – – – –▶ : A player running

The Photographs

The players used throughout the book to demonstrate techniques are Liverpool's John Barnes and Tony Adams of Arsenal and England; also Queen's Park Rangers goalkeeper David Seaman in the section on goalkeeping.

How the Game Began

Somewhere, many centuries ago, someone kicked a round object with his foot and that was the start of the world game called 'football'. No one knows where it happened or when. Experts have said football started in Greece, China, Mexico and the Roman Empire but there is no real evidence.

In the Middle Ages in England, a kind of football was played in the towns and villages with scores of young men taking part. There were no rules and injuries were so prevalent that several kings, including Richard II and Henry IV, banned it. In the rough form of street football the hands were used and every effort was made to wrestle the ball off whoever had possession of it.

The next significant development was when someone decided that it was beneficial to pass the ball to a colleague, but that came centuries later. Even in the 1860s, when the public schools had given the sport its first set of rules, football was still a dribbling game. Hacking, or kicking at an opponent, was outlawed around this time and was replaced by tackling, another art which came naturally to English players.

The esteem in which English football is held around the world today stems from the way the English developed football into an organised sport in which people of all classes can take part. The English did not invent football but they turned it into a recognisable game. A group of fourteen Cambridge University students drew up the first rules in 1848 and that was followed by the setting up of the Football Association in 1863 at the Freemasons' Tavern in Lincoln's Inn Fields, London.

At the first meeting of the newly-formed FA a revised set of rules was drawn up which forbade players from carrying the ball. The street game of the earlier centuries was split in two, with those wanting to handle the ball starting a new game called 'rugby'.

In 1871 it was decided that each team would be limited to eleven players. There were ten outfield players and a new rule had been brought in to govern the role of the eleventh man, the goalkeeper.

Most of the changes that followed took place in England: the FA Cup in 1872, the start of League football in 1888 and the formation of clubs, many professional, all over the country. The Industrial Revolution provided the wealth for rich men to pay for the new grounds that were needed. Football became basically a working-class sport again and Leagues were formed in every town and hamlet to provide the workers with recreation on a Saturday afternoon.

By the turn of the century, British sailors were taking the game abroad and soon it became a world-wide sport with millions of players and many millions of spectators. In 1930, an international body called FIFA launched the first World Cup and it was won in Uruguay by the home country. England did not take part. It was not until 1950 that England eventually agreed to enter.

In the mid-Thirties, the FA decided that it would be useful to do some coaching. They decided that football could be taught like any other skill or subject and so they set up courses. The arrival of Walter Winterbottom at the FA after the Second World War provided the initiative to make the FA's courses worthwhile and soon a coaching scheme was set up which was copied throughout the world.

English football owes a tremendous debt to the visionary Winterbottom, a man whose services were sought after throughout the world. Standards of play improved after he set up the nationwide coaching scheme.

'Coaching' is another word for teaching. Any player, young or old, will get better if he is taught properly the individual skills and team understanding. A good coach harnesses instinctive natural ability, showing the player how to get the best out of it.

Natural talents like Stanley Matthews, Tom Finney, Pelé and Diego Maradona will always thrust themselves into prominence but there is no player who did not become a better player by being taught an aspect of the game he did not know much about before.

At the latest count, 158 countries belong to FIFA and half the world's population watch a World Cup Final on television. No other sport enjoys such popularity. Football holds such an attraction because it is so simple, and so inexpensive to play. The best ideas about how to play it are simple ones and if coaching could be simplified into a single sentence, it would be: 'Trying to get two players from your side against one from the other team, or 2 v.1.' When that happens near goal, a goal will follow . . . or should.

The Pitch

The most important part of the game of football is the pitch. Yet although much time is devoted to talking about the state of the pitch in cricket and other sports, in soccer it is virtually ignored by many. But not by the players.

When they visit a ground, the first thing they will investigate is the pitch. They will inspect it and come back with their impressions. At times they may be discouraged by its condition, claiming it is too bumpy or lacking in grass, or maybe too hard. The coach will try to ensure that they are not about to use that as an excuse, telling them, 'It is the same for both sides.'

If the pitch is flat and has a good surface, the players can be confident that their skills will flourish. Good players will have their heads up, looking for passing options as they control the ball. But if it is an uneven surface with the ball bouncing awkwardly, they will have to look down at the ball and the standard of play will deteriorate.

Up to twenty or so years ago, the condition of all pitches followed a similar pattern. At the start of the season they were well-grassed and firm. Lightweight players would be made to look good. It would be more of a passing game. By November and December, however, the pitches would be muddy and heavy, with the grass rapidly disappearing down the middle. The ball would be passed longer. In January and February, pitches would be frozen and hard and the game became even longer. With the chance of defenders slipping and making mistakes, the ball would be sent into the opposing half as quickly as possible.

The players who impressed at the start of the season were much less impressive towards the end. Stronger, more physical players were the ones who were in the forefront. Just as Boris Becker is better on grass and Ivan Lendl better on hard courts, so some players prefer firm pitches and others surfaces which have a 'give' in them.

Improved methods of treating pitches have meant that surfaces are much better today. No longer are there bare patches up the middle. Sand-slitting, the process of driving strips of sand into the soil, has helped drainage so that the pitch dries more quickly. Grounds at Everton, Liverpool, Nottingham Forest, Ipswich and Wimbledon have first-class pitches and others which used to have problems, like Tottenham Hotspur and Derby County, are now much improved.

The advent of under-soil heating has accelerated this trend by eliminating the ravages of heavy frosts. The clubs who have spent up to £100,000 on under-soil heating, like Everton, Liverpool, Spurs and Arsenal, have inevitably benefited at the expense of those whose matches have been postponed, causing a last-minute rush of games at the end of the season. It is amazing that more clubs do not invest in under-soil heating. For the price of an average player, they would gain many advantages.

There are three main types of under-soil heating: 1) Hot water pipes similar to the central heating in a house. 2) Pipes with small holes which blow out hot air, or when there has been heavy rain, suck in moisture and dispose of it. 3) Electric wires like those of an electric blanket under the surface.

For those countries that do not have a mid-season break, under-soil heating seems the only answer. Eventually, indoor football stadiums will be built in Britain and all the problems caused by the weather will disappear. The Americans have shown it is possible to build such stadiums but the British have been slow to construct new ones. The last major ground to be built was Wembley in 1923.

In the World Cup in Spain the standard of pitches was first class, but in Mexico four years later there were complaints from almost every competing country about the poor quality of the playing surfaces. In Mexico the pitches were spongy and the grass was too long. At the Aztec Stadium, where the main games including the Final took place, badly-filled holes presented problems to the players and Peter Shilton made an official complaint about the state of one goal-mouth.

The next World Cup in Italy in 1990 should present fewer problems because the standard of pitches there is extremely high. But the higher the level of the game, the better the pitches should be.

Artificial pitches

Most professional players do not like playing on artificial pitches, and it is difficult to see surfaces other than grass having a future except for training purposes.

The problem is balance. On an artificial pitch, players find it hard to perform their skills such as crossing the ball at speed, and when the surface is wet it is virtually impossible for them to retain their balance.

Four clubs – Queen's Park Rangers, Luton, Oldham and Preston – installed artificial pitches for economic reasons and others were poised to follow their example until the Football League imposed a three-year moratorium which expires in 1990. The economic argument makes sense but the playing one does not.

The artificial pitches do encourage accurate passing to feet, and the ball runs truly. It is also fair to say that some ball skills will improve as a result. However, so many other aspects of the game suffer. Tackling, for example, is difficult to execute. Players who slide into the tackle will suffer burns which, unlike grass burns, take up to a month to heal.

Playing regularly on such a pitch gives the home side a great advantage when an opposing team used to playing on grass visits them. The home players will be more used to the bounce, which will be greater than on a grass pitch, and also the pace of the ball which is quicker.

The most significant fact about artificial pitches is that many countries in the Middle East have forsaken them and laid grass pitches instead. The rich owners of the clubs in those countries feel an artificial surface is no substitute for the real thing.

The Ball

Before a Football League match, the referee is given three balls by the home club to examine. He chooses the one he wants to use in the match, having satisfied himself that it conforms to the regulations for size and pressure. He will pass the ball through a ring to test its circumference and check the pressure with a pressure gauge.

These days the leather ball has a plastic coating which does not absorb water and attract mud like the old leather balls. The modern ball is livelier and bouncier and tends to swing about more in the air. But it is consistent and better to kick, especially with long passes.

Goalkeepers do not like balls that wobble about in flight, and it has to be admitted that some of today's balls do dip and swerve without reason. They are a goalkeeper's nightmare.

When Wolves were at their peak in the Fifties, the story went that their trainer used to soak the old leather type of ball used in those days in a bucket of water to make it heavier and more suited to the style of his team's players.

The ball of that era had a thick lace which could cause injury when heading. The modern ball has no lace, just a pin-hole for the valve. The rival companies vie with each other in coming up with new designs and colours. The higher the altitude at which the game is played, the more quickly the ball will pass through the air. In Mexico, goal-keepers found this a problem but perhaps not as difficult a one as they first feared.

The Boot

When I first started playing football, boots were made of thick leather which stretched above the ankle and had solid toe-caps. Professional players used to buy a size below their real size and squeeze them on to their feet, then stand in a hot bath to allow the leather to expand. That way they were able to mould the boot to suit the size of their feet. But it could be an uncomfortable process and it took a long time to wear boots in properly.

Some players used to have their boots especially made, but the only British player I know who does that these days is Ray Wilkins. It is a more common practice in Italy.

Today's players buy their boots or have them given and are able to put them on and go straight out to play. Modern boots are smaller, much lighter and easier on the feet.

The professional player has three types of boot: the studded boot with screw-in studs which can be changed to suit conditions and is used mainly on dry grass pitches, the moulded rubber boot for hard grounds, and the boot with a pimpled sole suitable for use on artificial pitches or training grounds. Today's boot is low-cut around the ankle and has a soft toe-cap. There is a greater chance of injury but players prefer the lightness and comfort. They believe they can 'feel' the ball better.

The lightest boots I ever saw were those worn by Stanley Matthews when I first played with him in 1959. They were almost paper thin and lasted no more than half a dozen games.

Most of today's boots last a season or more. The studded boot has three lengths of stud – short (about quarter of an inch), medium (half an inch) and long (three quarters of an inch). The studs can be made of leather, rubber, aluminium, plastic or similar material and must be solid. They have to be round and not less than half an inch in diameter. Studs which are roughed up on concrete or hard surfaces on the way to the pitch can cause serious injuries, and the referee has the power to send off players whose equipment does not conform to the strict regulations. Linesmen run their hands along a player's studs to ensure that they are not dangerous before he goes on to the field.

During the 1986 World Cup a number of players who play in the Italian League, including Ray Wilkins, Mark Hateley and the Italian team, had to change their studs because they were too pointed and less than half an inch in diameter. Officials have a piece of equipment, a metal bar with a hole in it, to make the necessary tests.

The usual practice is to have six studs in a studded boot but in recent years some manufacturers have added an additional stud under the big toe to improve balance. Others have a longer stud under the heel, a medium-sized stud in the middle of the boot and a shorter stud at the front to give a better balancing effect.

Moulded rubber boots are used to train in, to play on hard pitches and also frozen pitches. Moulded rubber studs can be thinner, three-eighths of an inch, providing there are no fewer than ten on the sole.

There are various types of boots suitable for artificial pitches, ranging from those with small, pimpled studs to those with suction holes.

(*Opposite*) The footballer's kit.

What length of stud?

It is advisable for the manager or coach to inspect the pitch before the match begins, so that he can help his players choose their footwear. The general rule is: the softer the ground, the more likely it is players will want to use a longer stud. The drier and harder the surface, the shorter the stud.

Parts of the pitch will vary. The ground could be hard through the middle and soft on the wings. One side could be partially frozen while the other side, open to the sun, may be softer. All aspects have to be taken into consideration and the player has to make up his own mind.

Many players wear an inner sole for extra comfort and that is something to be recommended. Care should be taken over lacing the boot. Laces should not be too thick and bulky, or too thin. Nor should the knot be tied to the side of the foot. The best place for the knot is high up on the centre of the foot, an area which is used less. Extravagant bows are not advised. It is easy to catch a stud in the bow, which can result in twists and strains.

Even with today's improved design of boots, blisters can be a problem, and I recommend rubbing soft soap or Vaseline on the inside of the sock around the affected area. If the boot is ill-fitting, or the laces are not properly tightened, friction can be caused, leading to blisters. Often players wear two pairs of socks.

Some boot manufacturing companies have introduced boots which have a raised heel to guard against heel injuries, but the rubbing they sometimes produce can cause tendinitis.

Few professional players buy their own boots. They are usually supplied by one of the big companies like Adidas, Puma or Gola and are paid a commission for wearing them. A player like Diego Maradona can earn up to £500,000 for a boot contract but the average reward for an international player is England is around £10,000 a season, with a run-of-the-mill First Division player getting up to £5,000, and players lower down the scale, who are not so likely to appear on television, considerably less. This explains why it is sometimes possible to see players stop and tie their laces up in big matches. They know the cameras are likely to be on them and they are giving their boot supplier a free plug around the world. Pelé once delayed the start of an important World Cup match by performing this trick!

Players should look after their own boots, even the top players, because they are the tools of their trade. The modern boot needs the minimum of care. Unlike the old-fashioned leather-soled boot which used to get caked in mud and grass, the modern plastic-soled boot does not collect much mud or grass except around the studs. It is advisable for players to have a scrubbing brush and a bucket available to brush off their boots when they come in at the end of a training session. They should then hang them up in a warm room to dry. Boots should not be put in front of a fire or radiator. That only shrinks the leather.

It is not necessary to apply dubbin, but the occasional use of black polish is recommended to help appearances. A player who wants to look smart is more likely to be stimulated and alert. One player in my time who always took the greatest care of his boots was the former Arsenal and Scotland centre-half Ian Ure. He even used to put shoe-trees in his boots to help them keep their shape. In contrast, Everton's Peter Reid tended to be indifferent about the condition of his boots and was constantly ribbed by other players as a result.

Professional clubs have a kit man to see the boots are in their proper place in the boot room and to look after the kit. With the England team, Norman Medhurst, one of the trainers, takes care of the match boots and the players look after their training boots. One of Norman's tasks is to repaint the identification marks on boots which signify the trademark of the maker. At international level, that is very important!

(*Below*) Steve Bruce, centre-half for Manchester United, tying up his bootlaces.

Protecting the Legs

Players who go on the field without shin-pads are taking an unnecessary risk. Any manager or coach should discourage his players from ignoring the advantages of protecting their legs.

Some players, like Alvin Martin, Garry Thompson and Hans-Peter Briegel, say they find pads uncomfortable and restricting. But that should not be the main consideration. After all, football is a contact sport and each player owes it to his team-mates not to court injury.

Fortunately, most players recognise the need for protection, and up to seventy-five per cent of League players now wear a type of pad which also incorporates an ankle protector. It fits over the ankles like a sock and the pad is made of plastic rods joined together rather in the mould of the Victorian woman's stays. The cost is high for a parks player, around £12, but I feel the outlay is warranted. The latest design is made of a hard, lightweight material which has air trapped in pockets and is known as the 'Air Pad'. With the modern style of boot, there is no protection for the ankle and this device makes up for that. The pace of the game is faster than it used to be and it is easier for players to receive knocks on the ankle. Wearing protection minimises the risk of injury.

During the 1986 World Cup, FIFA insisted that players played with their shirts inside their shorts, and socks not round the ankles. No one likes to see scruffy-looking players whether it is in the parks or at Wembley. In the France v. Italy match, Luis Fernandez, the French midfield player, was ordered off the pitch by the referee because his socks were rolled round his ankles. Fernandez was not allowed back until his socks were tied up in the accepted manner.

A wide bandage type of tie-up is recommended, not a lace which cuts into the leg and restricts circulation. The bandage should be tied in a knot at the back of the leg, not at the front or side.

Clothing

Shirts and shorts have changed over the years, mainly in design, but the basic format remains. Shorts have become shorter and shirts more colourful.

English players who have played in Italy, like Trevor Francis and Ray Wilkins, usually wear singlets under their shirts. They say Bri-Nylon shirts do not soak up the sweat in the heat and they need to wear a cotton undervest or singlet. In hot climates or at the start of the English season, cotton shirts are therefore recommended in preference to Bri-Nylon. In England it is usually only the goalkeeper who wears a singlet, but it is a matter of personal preference.

Most top-class players wear underpants or swimming trunks under their shorts rather than the traditional jock-strap. This again depends on the individual.

In the 1986 World Cup the players had numbers on the sides of their shorts, Celtic style, and that is a good idea because it is not always possible to see the numbers on their backs. It would also be useful to see numbers on the side of the arm.

Some players at lower levels wear chains and medallions but they ought not to because Law IV (see page 195) prohibits the wearing of anything that could be dangerous to an opponent. That includes all kinds of jewellery.

Preparation for a Match

If a player normally goes to bed at eleven, it is not a good idea for him to go to bed an hour earlier the night before a match. He should follow his usual routine. Some players ask for sleeping tablets to help them sleep, but this is not a practice to be recommended at any level of the game.

The pattern at most professional clubs where advice is given to players about diet, is that high protein food should be eaten at the start of the week, with a switch to high carbohydrate food at the end of the week. Fish, pasta, chicken and plenty of fruit and vegetables are essential parts of any athlete's diet.

Most footballers do not give enough attention to their diet. They tend to eat too many things that are bad for them, like hamburgers, crisps, fatty foods and sweet things. Yet studies in other sports have shown that players can perform better and outlast their opponents if their diet is controlled. In tennis, Martina Navratilova and Ivan Lendl are outstanding examples of athletes who eat a mainly carbohydrate diet of pasta, rice and wholemeal bread.

There have been many instances of players lacking stamina who have been given extra training, only to find they deteriorate still further. Closer investigation shows that the fault lies with their diet. Tony Adams was an example of this in his early days with Arsenal. He ate far too much steak and chips and junk food, and his performance only improved when he switched to a diet of mainly fish, chicken, vegetables and fruit. Micky Hazard had similar difficulties when he was with Tottenham.

Footballers have traditionally eaten steak and chips, and only in recent years has it been established that meat, which takes a long time to digest, is not good as a pre-match meal. The idea that steak was helpful developed after the visit of the Hungarians in 1953 when they beat England 6–3. Ferenc Puskas and his colleagues consumed large quantities of steak, and it was thought that this was one of the reasons for their success. But it is more likely that they ate so much meat because they could not get steak in Budapest at the time!

The night before a match the ideal food for a footballer is pasta, bread and potatoes – high carbohydrate foods which provide energy. On the day of the game, some form of exercise is recommended in the morning, either a brief fifteen-minute walk or some light jogging. Some players will prefer a slightly more strenuous warm-up; Watford's players make it part of their routine.

The best time for the pre-match meal is three hours before kick-off and ideally it should consist of cereals (such as cornflakes or rice krispies), scrambled or poached egg on toast and fruit – foods that provide energy and that can be easily digested. Tea or coffee can be served. Up to kick-off time, the player should aim to drink as much fluid as he finds comfortable, squashes or electrolyte drinks which will delay the dehydration process in the latter stages of the game.

Forty minutes before the start, players should begin stretching exercises which loosen up muscles and prepare them for the match. These can continue on the pitch in the warm-up period. It is important to work up a sweat. Some British players are self-conscious when they exercise on the pitch – unlike the South Americans and many Continentals who seem to relish it – but there is no reason why they should be: it is part of their job.

Many of today's professionals insist on having a warm bath before a match. They believe it helps the loosening-up process, particularly if they have been suffering from a minor injury. Bryan Robson and Peter Shilton are two players who follow this practice.

(*Below*) Brian Stein, striker for Luton Town, warming up.

Warm-ups

It is absolutely vital for all footballers over the age of sixteen to undertake a programme of warm-up exercises before taking part in a match. Ideally this should last about twenty minutes. To start kicking a ball without stretching the leg muscles is inviting trouble.

The exercises should be done firstly in a stationary position and then while running. No athlete goes out and runs without warming up and that should also apply to a footballer. It is a boring prospect but an essential one.

Starting from the feet upwards, the ankle can be rotated in either direction and stretched up and down to loosen the muscles and ligaments. Then stretch the calves and thighs by bending and kicking the legs up from behind, so the heel almost touches the buttocks. The process can be prolonged by the player grabbing hold of his foot and holding it for a few seconds (*Fig. 1*).

Then comes the exercising of the groin and hamstring muscles by putting one leg wide to the side, the other one in a withdrawn position and holding the position to the count of five (*Fig. 2*).

This can be followed by trunk rotation and touching of the toes to make the back and stomach muscles more supple. The shoulders should be lifted in turn and the elbows worked across the chest (*Fig. 3*). Care should also be taken to ensure that the neck is properly prepared, rotating the head in alternate circular motions, lifting it back and pressing it down.

It is preferable for these exercises to be

Fig. 1

Fig. 2

Fig. 3

performed in a warm atmosphere, and afterwards they can be followed by jogging and running on the pitch. The routine of kicking the legs back and touching the heels is an important one. After a few short sprints the player will be ready to work with the ball for a short time.

Kicking-in should be left to the specialist who is warming up the goalkeeper. The other players should work on passing the ball to each other and concentrating on movement rather than merely standing around.

The Psychology of Winning

To win, a footballer has to have the desire to win. He can have ability, skill and a good technique but his attitude of mind is also of crucial importance. The team whose players have an aggressive spirit will win more than a team whose players do not have it to such a degree.

In general, English teams have a more competitive attitude than many foreign teams. It is one of the reasons why English football is so popular on television around the world. Neither side wants to lose, so it is a fight to the very end.

Team spirit

Although matches are frequently won by the actions of an individual, football remains a team game and the teams which are more successful are those which have a good team spirit and understanding. Good sides are those that act as a strong unit, with every player working unselfishly for all his colleagues.

The essence of the success of the Arsenal 'Double' team was that the squad was made up of a number of strong personalities who worked well together. They encouraged each other and took criticism in the right manner.

The attitude needed to make a team a winning one is summed up by the phrase, *All for one, one for all.* It also helps if the players like and respect each other.

Skill can be taught, effort and attitude cannot, which is why the coach has to try to motivate those who are unable to motivate themselves. This is why Bryan Robson has been such an outstanding captain of England. His spirit affects the other players. 'Let's be first, let's win it,' he will say. Peter Reid has the same qualities, so does Terry Butcher. They want to be winners, and even if they have played well but lost, they are still downcast.

The players must think like boxers who know that there is an opponent in the next dressing-room – someone who wants to knock them out. They must realise that they will not get through on skill alone.

Some players will not talk about winning. They will talk about an aspect of passing, or something else other than the paramount object, which is winning. The more of this type of player in the side, the less chance of success.

George Best had more skill than possibly any other player born in the United Kingdom but most important, like all sportsmen, he knew why he went out on the pitch . . . to win.

It is often said that English football is too competitive, particularly at schoolboy level, that youngsters are taught to compete before they learn how to kick the ball properly. This may be a fair criticism at youth level, and eleven-a-side matches below the age of ten or eleven years are not to be encouraged. The basics have to be mastered first. But later on, that quality known as 'the right attitude' is essential to any player. No player who is happy losing a game can ever be a good player. One of Liverpool's greatest attributes must be that they never think they are going to lose.

Which way to kick?

Which way should a captain decide to kick if he wins the toss?

Some pitches, like Oxford's and Sheffield Wednesday's, have a slope and it will be an advantage if the coach knows the preference of the home side when it comes to winning the toss. Oxford, for example, like kicking down the hill. If they are denied that privilege, it might affect their players. It can also affect crowds. Liverpool traditionally like attacking the 'Kop' end at Anfield in the second half, but whenever I took a team there I told my captain to make them attack the 'Kop' end in the first half if he won the toss. A coach has to seek to exploit every psychological ploy!

The captain should also take account of the direction of the wind. In previous years, the policy was always to kick with the wind in the first half to try and get the lead and in case it dropped in the second half. Now the opposite is the case. Teams like to combat the wind when they are fresh and use it to their advantage in the second half when their legs begin to tire.

It is often better to play against the wind than with it because long passes into the back of the defence will hold up, enabling forwards to reach the ball before it goes out of play or into the hands of the goalkeeper.

A further consideration is the position of the sun. A captain may elect for his team to play with their backs to the sun so that it is shining in the goalkeeper's face. This ploy is especially effective in the winter when a bright, low sun can be at times quite blinding.

Confidence

Some years ago the former Manchester City and England player Mike Summerbee suddenly lost his form and confidence. Malcolm Allison, who was the manager at Maine Road at the time, tried everything to help him overcome his problems.

He gave him extra training and had him in his office to talk it out. Nothing worked. One day Allison tried another tack. 'Summerbee is finished,' he told some of the other players. The players, as was intended, passed on his comments to Summerbee.

Summerbee was livid and went to Allison's house to see him. 'I'll show you what I can do,' he shouted. In the next match, Summerbee was back to his best form. His pride had been hurt and he responded in the way Allison had hoped.

Such basic psychology may not work every time. Often it does not. Encouragement is still the best way of instilling or restoring confidence, and a method I used on occasions was to invite the player to let me, as his manager, assume responsibility for what was going wrong in his game.

If a winger was no longer beating his full-back, for instance, and was frightened to make the effort to do so, I would call him in and say, 'Don't take any notice of what anyone is saying. I want you to take the fellow on. If it doesn't work, you can say it's down to me. Tell them that you're carrying out my instructions.'

If the player does not then make the effort, he will not succeed. Similarly with strikers. If they are having a bad time, they will tend to hide. But the only way for them to play themselves out of their bad spell is to keep trying to hit the target. If they do not try, they will not succeed. 'Never be afraid of failure,' is one of my many sayings.

The player who does not want to assume responsibility is of little use to his team. He must be urged to keep trying what he is good at and eventually his form will return.

Another ploy to restore confidence is something called 'visualisation'. Sometimes I would say to a player who was struggling, 'Imagine you are Michel Platini,' (or some other world-class player). 'How do you think he prepares for a game?' Then I would suggest, 'Why don't you try that? Think of what he is best at and imagine yourself doing that.' By persuading them to think of themselves in terms of another player, I was able to help them and make them forget their depression.

If a team is a losing side, it will be full of players lacking in confidence. The reverse is true with a winning side. If results are poor, it is a downward slide and every defeat adds more self-doubt, more gloom.

It is invaluable if one of the players in the team has unshakeable confidence because he can help gee the others up. Most great players have it. Peter Shilton has it and so does Graeme Souness. Billy Wright, Johnny Haynes and Dave Mackay had it. They were all uplifting players, players you could not imagine playing in a losing side. They had an air of invincibility about them.

The test of failure is what you do in the next game. The man who comes back to win is the one with the right approach. Frank McLintock was an outstanding example at Arsenal. He had appeared in a losing FA Cup Final with Leicester and a losing

(*Opposite*) Mike Summerbee in pensive mood when he was at Manchester City. Malcolm Allison's trick of using psychology helped him to regain his form.

League Cup Final with Arsenal at Wembley but withstood it all to emerge a winner.

When a player has lost confidence he should be careful to whom he goes for advice. Too many people will be willing to tell him things that will not benefit him. He should go to someone who will be honest and realistic.

In cricket, confidence can be measured. A batsman in a poor spell can look at his scores, or a bowler can assess his figures. But in football, a player whose confidence has deserted him can be hidden by a team's good results. The coach has to be honest with him and seek him out to offer help.

The player needs encouragement and objective advice. And he needs to keep working at his game.

Get the ball!

When a player is having a bad game he tends not to want the ball for fear of making more mistakes. This is a negative attitude. It is accepting that he cannot do anything about his troubles.

When a player is like this and the crowd is criticising him, I tell him: 'Get the ball! You might make a mess of it again but that doesn't matter because you are having a bad game anyway. But if you do something good with it, you are turning the corner. Perhaps people will remember that pass and not the poor ones earlier.'

Getting the ball is the only way of getting back into a good game again.

Half-time

Half-time is a vitally important time for a manager or coach. It is the time when he earns his money if he is a professional. As the players sit down and drink tea – which is the usual drink at most clubs, poured from an already sugared jug – he will first satisfy himself about the seriousness of injuries and whether the afflicted player or players are fit to continue.

Managers will rarely give praise at half-time. If they do, they might convey the impression to the players that the job is already done. Complacency might creep in. Instead, the manager will examine the reasons why his side has done well and insist that the tactics which have brought success continue to be used for the remaining forty-five minutes.

If the team is losing, he will dwell on the reasons why they are losing, such as whether a certain player is not being picked up, in which areas the other side is causing damage and whether players are supporting and helping each other enough.

He must not indulge in generalities. He must confront individual players. I remember once at Leeds when I was coach, I said to the team at half-time, 'You're not getting your tackles in.' Billy Bremner, who could hardly be accused of that, replied, 'Who isn't getting their tackles in?' It taught me a lesson. The coach has to name names.

If players are not giving enough effort, the manager or coach has to sort it out. Violent arguments in dressing-rooms at half-time are not as common as is supposed. But there are occasions when voices are raised and discussion becomes heated.

Good players will accept criticism and respond with points of their own. A coach ought to encourage a response from players, but must remember that ten minutes at half-time is not long and he must be the person to get things said, not the players.

How often does the stimulus of what is said at half-time bring about victory in the second half? A tactical change can win a match, or a gee-up to greater effort can produce the desired effect. One occasion, I can remember, when I think I influenced the result, was in an FA Cup semi-final against Stoke. Arsenal were 2–0 down at half-time. I made some tactical changes, including giving Charlie George a new role, and the team produced a recovery which enabled Arsenal to draw 2–2. They went on to win the replay.

A coach will rehearse what he wants to say at half-time in the few minutes before the referee brings the players off. Some even make notes on a pad. The tendency these days is for the coach to sit in the stand in the first half, to get an overall picture of the match, and sit in the dug out in the second half, to be closer to the play, to make tactical changes and offer encouragement.

Most home dressing-rooms at League clubs will have a tactical board displayed where the manager or coach can chalk his ideas and set pieces. He will run through these ideas before a match, and if his instructions are not being carried out, will repeat them at half-time. Unfortunately, when his team are away from home, there are no tactical boards!

The End of a Game

Players will want some reaction from the manager or coach at the end of a game. If they have played well and won, they like being congratulated but they will be just as anxious to be given a frank appraisal of their performance. The appraisal should be honest and constructive. Having been told he didn't play well, a player wants to know why.

Many managers are so worked up that they express their feelings strongly once the players are back in the dressing-room. They will rant and rave for a few minutes and leave the players to think over what has been said. Other managers prefer to make a few general comments and continue with the post-match analysis on the Monday morning, or the next time the players are together.

One aspect of play the manager can never ignore is the amount of effort put in by the team. If someone has not tried hard enough, the manager has to let him know about it. Lack of effort is inexcusable. A coach can do something about improving skills but he can do little about a player's willingness to work. Some players do not require a stimulus. Others are lazy and need prodding all the time.

Often there is a reason why a player is below his best. He could have a family or personal problem. He might not be one hundred per cent fit. It is up to the coach to talk it over with him and help him.

Most rows in dressing rooms are over attitudes. Effort is just as important as skill. That cannot be stressed enough.

At many clubs, even the biggest, there are plunge baths which the players use. Experts have said it is unhygienic for as many as thirteen dirty footballers to bathe in the same water, but there is the counterbalancing factor that the communal bath is good for team spirit! It is a great place to have a chat, sit and relax.

Some players will prefer to use a shower or, if there are any, individual baths. But showers are not as relaxing. At some clubs there are facilities to provide a soothing massage, and some players like this, either before or after a game.

The accepted practice in football is to have an alcoholic drink or two after a match. While it might be true that this helps the players to relax, it must be said that the consumption of alcohol, particularly at this time, is not a good idea. Alcohol helps to dehydrate the body, it means that the recovery process is delayed. It is not therefore surprising that often when players report for training on the Monday, they are feeling tired.

If a player needs to drink, it should be done on the Sunday, by which time the body has recovered.

Two of the greatest players ever produced in Britain, Stanley Matthews and Tom Finney, never drank. Matthews drinks only water even today. He played his last competitive match when he was fifty and Finney retired from First Division football at the age of thirty-seven. This only goes to show that the players who have long careers are those who take care of their bodies.

It is difficult to convince young players of the truth of this argument. They are easily persuaded that it is a macho thing to drink to excess after matches. The price, a heavy one, is inevitably paid later.

Behaviour on the Field

With football today being challenged by so many other sports, it will only retain its premier position if the participants continue to enjoy it and the game is played in a good spirit. It is right that players should help each other with advice and support, but too much moaning, too much complaining to the referee can ruin the pleasure of the occasion, especially at the lower levels.

The emphasis should be on encouraging young players, not damaging their confidence by a constant stream of criticism. A competitive attitude is called for, but at the end of the game the players should be able to go up to each other and shake hands. They should also thank the referee and officials. This still happens after every Football League match but it is a point which is often overlooked in other games.

Showing joy when a goal is scored is part of the game but players running towards the spectators waving their arms about and making gestures is unnecessary. It can also provoke crowd trouble. The future of the professional game has been threatened by hooliganism and players must play their part in seeing that crowd problems are overcome, not exacerbated.

Kissing and cuddling is, in my view, an excess. Preferable is the procedure of the previous generation when colleagues would go up to the goalscorer and shake his hand.

In cricket and rugby no one used to argue with the umpire or referee, Sadly, that is changing, but it is an ideal that should also be sought in football. Right or wrong, the referee and his linesmen must be heeded and respected.

For a manager or coach to allow his players to keep questioning decisions is wrong. Fortunately, in recent years dissent has abated in League football and it is much less of a problem.

Referees are human and can make mistakes, just as footballers do – and players make them frequently. But we should all remember that without referees there would be no game. Some Leagues have had trouble recruiting referees because the atmosphere on the pitch in recent years has put off many potential candidates. Managers and coaches have the power to do something about this.

II

Playing the Game

Controlling the Ball

They say in football: 'He's got a good first touch,' or 'He's got a poor first touch.'

What they mean is that he has good, or poor, control. Good players in any sport give the impression of having plenty of time. Poor control in football means less time to select your pass, and under pressure a poor pass will result.

Control is only a means to an end, the end being a pass or shot at goal. In this country we admire the touch and control of the Continental players. It comes from endless practice time spent with the ball. The longer a player actually plays with the ball, the better his 'feel' for it.

The rules of proper control are:

1 Get in line with the ball early.

2 Select the controlling part of the body.

3 Withdraw that part on impact to cushion and take the pace out of the ball.

4 Control the ball to the side of the body so that it can be passed with a second touch.

The most common controlling technique is with the inside of the foot, mainly on passes along the ground, but it is also used a lot on knee-high balls. The essential part of this control is withdrawing the foot on impact and, in the same movement, placing the ball for the next action – a pass, a run with the ball or a shot. A point of great importance is that the head must come up on impact to look for the next move. Every

player should practise to get this technique perfect.

Points of Control

There are eleven parts of the body which can be used to control the ball – the inside, outside and front of each foot (six parts in all), each thigh, the chest, the midriff and the head. All these parts of the anatomy can be utilised, depending on where the ball is in relation to the receiver.

Trapping – the wedge trap

One of the most common methods of controlling a dropping ball is with the inside or outside of the foot (*Fig. 4*). The essential features are:

1 The foot should form a wedge with the ground, trapping the ball under it.

Fig. 4

(Opposite) Trapping and screening the ball with the inside of the foot
Although he is under pressure, Barnes keeps his eyes on the ball and his body virtually side on. Notice how his foot is well over the ball when he traps it.

2 Timing is vital. If it is not right, the ball will bounce away. Try and get the knee over the ball.

(*Right*) France's midfield player, Jean Tigana, shows how to control the ball with the outside of the foot while under pressure from Italy's Bruno Conti.

Trapping the ball with the outside of the foot
(*Below*) To turn to his right and away from the challenge, Barnes traps the ball with the outside of his right foot.

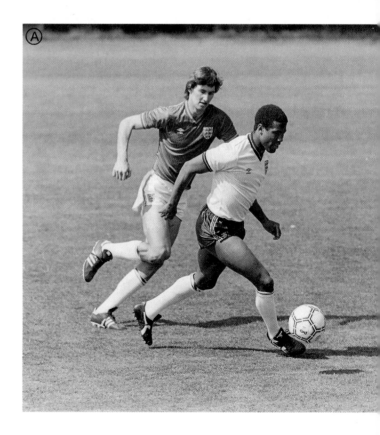

3 As with kicking the ball, because the weight is on one foot, the arms have to be spread out to provide the right balance.

4 Having controlled the ball, it should be quite natural to move away in the direction in which it has been trapped.

Trapping and controlling the ball with the outside of the foot

The same principles apply as for the wedge trap. The body leans to the right (assuming the player is trapping with the right foot to move to the right) and the right leg is crossed in front of the left. The knee should be slightly bent. Before controlling the ball, the player gives a dummy in the opposite direction to get away from marking.

Trapping and controlling the ball with the sole of the foot

The body has to be in a slightly crouching position facing the ball. The 'trapping' foot is raised about twelve inches from the ground with the toe pointing upwards to

Fig. 5

Fig. 6

Fig. 7

Fig. 8

give the wedge effect (*Fig. 5*). Depending on the speed of the ball, the receiver will be able to cushion it and push it a foot or two ahead to allow him to make his next move. If the ball is coming hard, the cushioning effect has to be greater.

Controlling a falling ball

A player may not have time to wait for the ball to reach the ground, and if it is bouncing and he is under challenge, he must be prepared to control it in the air. The kicking foot has to be much higher with the toe pointing upwards (*Fig. 6*).

Controlling a dropping ball with the front of the foot

More highly-skilled players seek to control the ball in the air before it reaches the ground and they use the front part of the boot, or the laces, to do it. The ball is 'caught' on the foot and dropped lightly to the ground (*Fig. 7*). It needs perfect timing to execute this skill. Just on the point of impact they withdraw the foot, taking the pace out of the ball, cushioning it to the floor.

Controlling a high ball with the inside of the foot

This is another 'quality' skill used by the best players. As the ball is dropping, they will not wait for it to land but will pull it down with the inside of the foot, taking it away from a defender's challenge (*Fig. 8*). Glenn Hoddle is particularly adept at dragging the ball away from opponents. The inside of the foot is most commonly used but strikers often have to use the outside of the foot.

Controlling the ball with the thigh

This is a skill for a dropping ball or awkward-height ball but can sometimes be

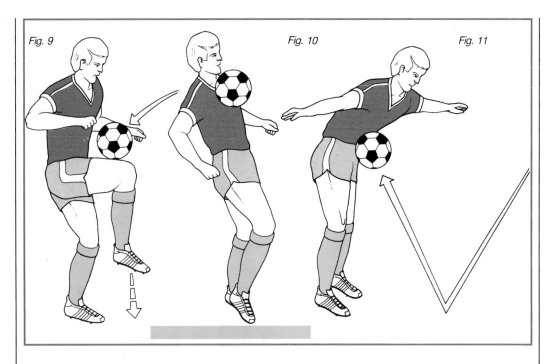

used to push the ball into the air to enable the other leg to volley the ball away. Alternatively, the ball can be directed downwards towards the ground with the thigh angled to cushion the ball (*Fig. 9*).

Controlling the ball with the chest

When a high ball is descending, a player under challenge may not have time to allow it to be trapped on reaching the ground, so an ideal solution is to chest the ball (*Fig. 10*). There are also passes which are too high to control with either foot but too low to head. Again, the chest is the answer.

Controlling the ball with the midriff

This skill is used to bring the waist-high bouncing ball quickly under control. The body must be leaning forwards from the hips, with the abdominal muscles tensed and

(*Above*) West Germany's Karl-Heinz Rummenigge shows how to take the ball just below the chin while being challenged by Argentina's Oscar Ruggeri. By leaning back, spreading the arms and bending the legs slightly, he has taken the pace out of the ball and is ready to move away from his opponent.

the arms and shoulders screening the ball. The arms must be spread for balance and to avoid handling (*Fig. 11*).

Controlling the ball with the head

This is a rarely used skill. It demands excellent timing with the player bending his knees at the moment of impact to allow his head to take the pace out of the ball. There will be a withdrawal motion of the neck muscles.

(*Right*) Scotland's Mo Johnston demonstrates a different way of controlling the ball with the chest, directing it down with his body leaning forward.

Passing or Delivering the Ball

During a game, a player should keep repeating the same question to himself: 'If I had the ball now, what would I do with it?'

Technique is a neglected aspect of football. Players rarely talk about it as, for example, golfers talk about their grip or their swing. Yet without a good technique, a footballer will never be fulfilled. He will never do his talents justice.

There are scores of players in the English First Division, some of whom have even played for their country, who have a poor technique. The ball will come to them and bounce away because they do not possess the skill to cushion it and make it their servant. When they kick the ball, their balance is wrong and the ball does not go where it is intended. The art of controlling the ball requires a sixth sense, a 'feel' for the ball. It comes from constant practice and dedication.

The best passers of the ball are inevitably those who have the best control because the player who can control the ball instantly makes time for himself, and time is space. If he has to trap the ball and then look up to see the passing options, defenders will have time to shut off his alternatives.

A good player will constantly be aware of the positions of colleagues and opponents alike, so that he knows what to do with the ball. This knowledge, plus the extra time he has won for himself by the quality of his control, will enable him to change his mind if he wants to try something different from his original plan. He will also be able to disguise his intentions.

Too many players are only anxious to talk about the result, not their performance in achieving it. Self-analysis is important. They should ask themselves the following questions more often:

'Why was my passing poor?'
'Why did I shoot over the bar?'
'Why don't I get the ball more often?'

They should do something about it themselves, not wait for the coach to advise them.

The role of the spectator is undervalued within football. It is a misconception to say that fans are only interested in the result. They want to see memorable moments of skill, like a back-heel from Socrates, or Maradona taking on five players and beating them all before scoring. They admire skill and are critical of a lack of it.

It is for these reasons that Glenn Hoddle was so popular at Tottenham and Charlie Nicholas at Arsenal. But they did not become players of such outstanding technique by being lazy. They worked hard at it.

I cannot emphasise enough the importance of practice. The more a player practises a skill, the more confident he will be of succeeding with it in a match. It becomes automatic, instinctive.

The basis of passing is movement. It can be summed up by the phrase, 'Give it and go.' For the player in possession to make a successful pass he has to have someone available to whom he can give the ball. That demands intelligent running off the ball. In the early post-war years, Tottenham were winners with a style christened 'push and run' by their manager Arthur Rowe. That principle of passing and then moving for a return pass has not changed.

Passing with the Inside of the Foot Along the Ground

The most common pass is the one with the inside of the foot. Its great virtue is that, properly executed, it will guarantee accuracy, but the drawback to it is that the range of the pass will be limited up to about twenty yards. The short pass with the inside of the foot is therefore more frequently used when a team adopts a short passing style, as on the Continent.

The essentials for a pass along the ground with the inside of the foot are:

1 The non-kicking foot must be placed alongside the ball, pointing in the direction of the pass, about four to six inches away.

2 The kicking foot must be at right angles to the body and also to the line of the ball, with the toes turned out, and the contact has to be in the centre of the ball.

3 The head must be kept still with the eyes looking down at the ball. The head must be over the ball to ensure it is kept down.

4 The ankle must be kept firm. (Ron Greenwood used to complain to Trevor Brooking that he flopped at the ball instead of striking it purposefully with a rigid ankle.)

The shape and balance of the body has to be right. The pace of the ball, or 'weight' as it is called, depends on the distance of the pass. Obviously, the longer the distance, the more power has to be applied. Knowing how much power to use is something which only comes with practice.

Bobby Moore, Denis Law, Alan Ball, Kenny Dalglish and Graeme Souness were all experts at this type of pass. The ball is usually played to feet but frequently it can be played into space. Liverpool are a side that uses the pass to put forwards in behind opponents. Other teams with a tradition of having a good inside-of-the-foot technique are Spurs and West Ham.

The disadvantages of the inside-foot pass are that it is not suitable for longer distances and it is not easy to make while running at speed. But it is the most accurate pass when a player has a good technique.

(*Left*) In his role as playmaker, Scotland's Graeme Souness probably made more passes with the inside of the foot than most of his contemporaries. Here he shows the advantage of being right over the ball. His balance is good, with arms slightly held out to help him, and his kicking foot not back too far. Perhaps his non-kicking foot is a little too close to the ball, but that is no handicap.

(*Below*) *Passing with the inside of the foot along the ground* As Adams approaches the ball, he has a quick look at the target then concentrates on the pass, pushing through the centre of the ball.

Passing the Ball into the Air with the Inside of the Foot (*Fig. 12*)

Similar principles to those for passing along the ground apply, with these adjustments:

1 The body has to lean back slightly to help the elevation of the ball.

2 The non-kicking foot should be turned in more towards the ball and should be slightly behind it.

3 The point of contact with the ball should be the centre of the bottom of the ball.

Passing the Ball in the Air on the Volley with the Inside of the Foot

This method is used for a first-time pass when the ball comes to the receiver in the air. The body has to be opened up to face the ball.

1 Turn the toe out and punch the ball with the instep.

(*Opposite*) *Passing with the inside of the foot into the air* Adams has his eyes on the ball and toe turned out as he kicks it from below.

2 To keep the ball down, concentrate on getting over it.

The Lob Pass

This is the pass used mainly by the back-four players to strikers upfield, or to the back of the opponents' defence. It is usually hit up to forty yards and requires a slightly different technique. The ball is contacted by the front of the foot, where the boot is laced up, and the inside of the toe scrapes the ground (*Fig. 13*). The leather on the modern boot can wear out if a player uses this type of pass regularly.

1 Contact must be made with the laces.

2 The non-kicking foot must be level with the ball but further away.

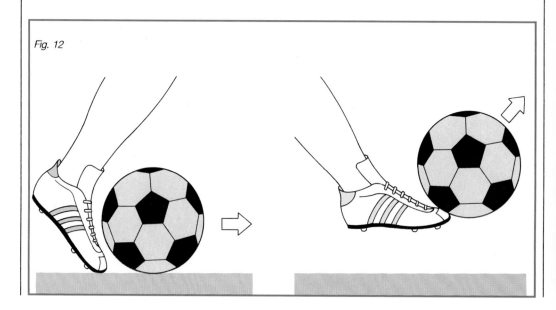

Fig. 12

Fig. 13

3 If the intention is to direct the ball straight down the pitch, the kicker must approach from an angle. If he approaches head on, the ball will go to the right with the natural swing of his kicking leg.

4 The backswing of the kicking leg must be more pronounced, with the heel almost touching the buttocks and the knee pointing towards the ball. The greater the pull-back of the leg, the more distance can be achieved.

5 The ball must be struck in the bottom half of the centre.

Midfield players use the lob pass to switch the play from one side of the field to the other. Full-backs should spend lots of practice time on this technique. They will use it the most.

(*Above*) Ray Wilkins, playing for England, delivers a long pass using the laces.

The Chipped Pass

The chipped pass is used mainly by midfield players and three of its finest opponents have been Danny Blanchflower, who could clear the head of a defender by a couple of inches to find a colleague, the West German Franz Beckenbauer and former French captain Michel Platini.

1 The foot must be jabbed under the ball, with contact being made by the inside of the big toe. (But great players like Beckenbauer used the outside of the foot, contacting the ball with the little toe.)

2 The head must be still and behind the ball.

3 The back-lift of the kicking foot must be minimal, from the knee.

4 The jabbing motion not only gives a sharp trajectory, but imparts back spin so that the ball holds up to await the arrival of the player whom the pass is intended to reach.

(*Above*) The Argentinian forward Jorge Burruchaga shows perfect balance as he chips the ball across the field in the 1986 World Cup Final. By leaning back he has enabled himself to give the ball the necessary altitude. With him is the West German defender Hans-Peter Briegel.

Passing with the Outside of the Foot or Front-Foot Passing

This is a valuable skill to have because it enables the player to pass while running. Unlike the pass with the inside of the foot, he does not have to check his stride.

He can also strike the ball longer distances. As the picture of Peter Reid shows, the

(*Left*) Peter Reid passing with the outside of the foot.

(*Below*) *Passing with the outside of the foot*
Barnes's toe is turned in as he punches the ball with the outside of his foot. The follow-through is short and low.

kicking foot has to be turned in so that it is almost pointing at the non-kicking foot and contact is made with the outside of the boot.

To get the ball to bend and spin, plenty of follow-through is needed.

Bending the Ball with the Inside of the Foot

This is a skill which is a vital part of the armoury of players who find themselves in positions to cross the ball. The angled cross behind defenders, swinging away from the goalkeeper, is one of the most dangerous passes in the game. Not many players are adept at it. Trevor Brooking was one of the best. It is also used to get the ball around and in the back of defenders, to players making through runs.

The technical points are:

1 The non-kicking foot has to be placed behind the ball.

2 The toe must be pointing straight ahead and contact made with the side of the big toe and foot.

3 A proper follow-through is important to ensure that spin is imparted to the ball, to get it to bend.

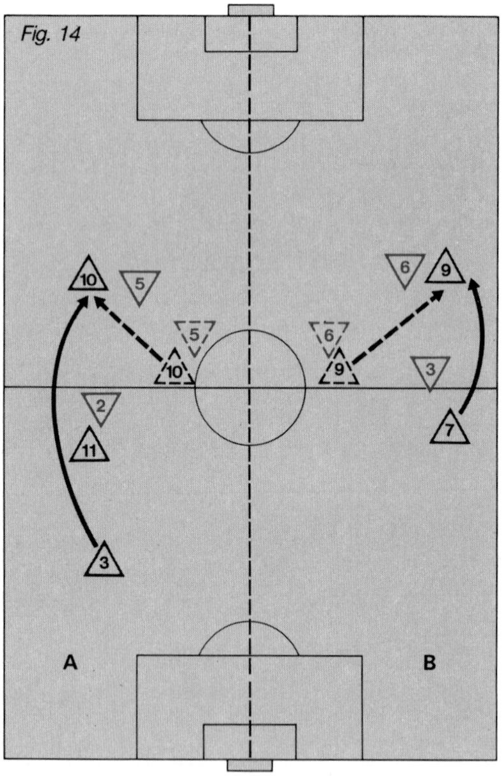

Bending the Ball with the Outside of the Foot (*Fig. 15*)

This is a skill which should be used more in English football. It is often seen in South America and on the Continent. Alan Woodward, the former Sheffield United winger, was a master of it and frequently employed it to take corner-kicks.

Fig. 14

Fig. 14 Two examples of passes, bending the ball with the inside of the foot
A The left-back △ bends his pass down the line into the striker's △ run.
B The outside-right △ bends his pass around the left-back ▽ into the striker's △ run.

Fig. 15

Like bending the pass with the inside of the foot, this pass is just as effective for passing around defenders and getting the ball in behind them.

Volleying the Ball (Kicking it before it Bounces)

There are many occasions in a game when it will be necessary to volley the ball. It is most important to get the body in the right position to attack the ball.

Volleying the ball straight

As Hugo Sanchez demonstrates, the head must be still and over the line of the ball. The arms should be spread to give balance and the kicking part of the front of the foot should be the laces, with the toes pointing down. With this volley you can get the ball to dip by dragging the foot up the face of the ball.

Volleying with the outside of the foot

This is a rare skill which Glenn Hoddle sometimes demonstrates to good effect. The foot has to be whipped outside the ball, imparting outspin.

The side-on volley

If the ball is directed to the side, instead of straight, the kicker has to be square-on to the ball. Assuming he is a right-footer, the left shoulder has to drop, pointing in the direction of the target so that he can lift his foot above the ball as he prepares to make contact (*Fig. 16*).

Fig. 16

(*Left*) Hugo Sanchez of Mexico volleying the ball straight during the 1986 World Cup Finals in Mexico City.

Half-volleys

A similar technique is used for kicking the ball as it is striking the ground. Timing is vitally important. Midfield players use this technique around the edge of the box when they shoot as the ball drops, and goalkeepers such as Ray Clemence and Peter Shilton have used it regularly to gain accuracy with kicks of up to fifty or sixty yards.

The Back-Heel

During the Mexico World Cup in 1986 the back-heel made a welcome comeback. Coaches always stress the importance of playing the ball the way you are facing but an element of surprise is useful, particularly if it is possible to disguise your intentions.

The former Brazilian captain Socrates was one of the leading exponents of the back-heel. The back-heel can be the simple one with the non-kicking foot placed alongside the ball and the kicking foot coming over the ball and flicking it backwards. Awareness of team-mates is vital. Back-heels to no one are the reason why it is safer for the player to play the way he is facing.

Alternatively, the player can use the cross-over approach. The left foot is placed inside the ball and the back heel is performed by the right foot coming across the non-kicking leg.

The Drive Pass

The technique for this type of pass, which is common in English football, is similar to that employed in the lob pass, with contact being made by the laces and the foot pointing downwards. The knee has to be over the ball. This pass is for distance and power, especially in dead-ball situations.

The Wall Pass

The 'wall pass' is used all over the pitch in build-ups and approach-play but it is most effective around the box to create scoring opportunities. Space is at a premium in this area and if the ball is played too heavily behind the last defender, the goalkeeper will have a good chance of getting it.

Fig. 17

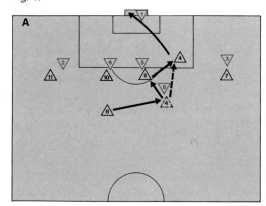

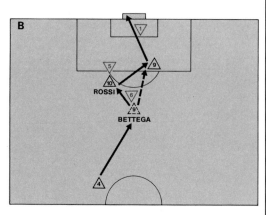

Fig. 17 Two examples of 'wall' passes
A Having received a pass from △, △ plays a 'wall' pass, using △ and bypassing two opponents ▽ and ▽, which enables him to get into the box for a shot at goal.

B The Italians use this type of 'wall' pass time after time. Bettega △ receives a pass with his back to the goal. With a deft touch, he helps the ball on into Rossi ⚠. He then spins for the return pass and a shot at goal.

The simplest way of getting through is by using a 'wall pass', so called because one player uses colleagues as a 'wall' to collect a rebound as he races through. The Continentals are particularly adept at it, but for some reason it is not employed as much as it should be here. Perhaps coaches do not spend enough time working on it.

Performed correctly, the wall pass on the edge of the box should produce a scoring opportunity. Bryan Robson has been one of England's best exponents of this tactic but the best example I can remember was the Paulo Rossi–Roberto Bettega combination in Argentina in 1978. Bettega had his back to goal, and as he played the ball to Rossi, he spun round to get the return pass. His awareness of the position of opposing defenders was first-rate.

The essentials of the wall pass are:

1 The player making the pass judges the distance when he passes the ball in to his team-mate. It must not be too close to the defender but not too far away either, about four feet.

2 The pass must be accurate. It must hit the man making the wall, preferably on the ground. But that is not vital. The receiving player can easily lay it off with his thigh, chest or head.

3 The player making the wall must time his move away from the defender. A last-second movement will drag the defender with him out of the space. He should make an angle, a better position to lay the ball off first-time. And he should aim to disguise his intention.

4 The return pass should be ahead of the runner, preferably on the ground but it can be in the air.

5 The runner having made the first pass must accelerate into the space for the return ball.

6 His composure at the end of the return pass will decide if he scores or not.

The wall pass used in wider positions

This type of pass is also used in wing-play, with the ball being played behind the full-, back. It is not so common as it used to be because full-backs today are much quicker than they were in the days of Matthews and Finney.

The Real Madrid players Alfredo di Stefano and Francisco Gento were outstanding practitioners of the art. At home, one of the leading exponents was George Graham when he played for Arsenal. He would disguise his intention by using the outside of his foot to flick the ball into the air for John Radford to run on to.

Formations of Play

In the beginning there was the ball and everyone used to run after it. That still happens in kick-abouts at primary school level! But as the game developed, systems of play evolved which enabled teams to make better use of their players. It became a passing and dribbling game instead of just a dribbling game.

Most tactical changes follow important International Matches. For example, the match which affected English football more than any other was at Wembley Stadium in 1953, when the final score was England 3 Hungary 6. Some of England's best-known tactical thinkers and innovators, including Walter Winterbottom, Ron Greenwood and Alf Ramsey (who was right-back in the England side that day) were there to see how the Hungarians exploited the weakness of England's WM formation by withdrawing a forward, Nandor Hidegkuti. Billy Wright, whom I used to watch at Molineux as a schoolboy, recalled: 'Nandor was the one who really won it.

'Others, like Puskas, got more credit but it was Nandor who pulled us all over the place and opened up the gaps. No one had put the centre-forward as deep as that before. Don Revie did the same thing later with Manchester City. It made a big difference to our game. No longer was it possible to take any notice of the numbers on players' shirts.'

Before the arrival of the Hungarians, the first foreign side to win at Wembley, every team in Britain used the same system – the so-called 'WM formation' with the players numbered in such a way that the spectators knew their positions without having to consult a programme.

The centre-forward was the number nine and led the attack, the centre-half was number five, the defensive wing-halves four and six and the inside-forwards eight and ten, with the full-backs two and three and the wingers seven and eleven. The goalkeeper did not have a number.

It meant that there were three players at the back, and as the Hungarians played with four forwards in a 4–2–4 formation, England's defenders were outnumbered.

Before the arrival of Herbert Chapman at Arsenal in the Twenties, most English sides played with only two defenders at the back, but the change of the offside law in 1925 (requiring only two players to be ahead of the ball and not three) caused a flood of goals, with Arsenal conceding seven in a match at Newcastle. This so upset the new signing Charlie Buchan that he persuaded Chapman to follow Newcastle's idea of moving the centre-half back alongside the full-backs. The centre-half then became the 'third back'. Arsenal went on to become the most dominant side in English football, and as happens when a team is successful, the others copied their methods. The WM formation survived for another twenty-eight years until it was killed off by Hidegkuti and his colleagues.

The predominant feature of WM was backbone, or strength through the middle. The key players were the goalkeeper, the centre-half and the centre-forward. Even today, managers will always look to have their best players in these positions.

The weakness of WM was that there was a shortage of cover in defence. If the left-back was threatened, for example, the right-back would come round behind the centre-half as cover. But that opened up plenty of space down the right, enabling a winger like

Jimmy Mullen to find his opposite number Johnny Hancocks with long cross passes at Wolves.

The switch to 4–2–4, with a second centre-half and a supporting centre-forward and a corresponding weakening of numbers in midfield (now only two) did not happen overnight in England. Many clubs were reluctant to abandon WM. It needed another International Match to affect the thinking of managers and coaches. That game was England 4 Spain 2 on a wet day at Wembley in 1960. Under Walter Winterbottom's guidance, England used a 4–2–4 system that day with Johnny Haynes and Bobby Robson as the two midfield players. The advantages of the system were that it provided an extra covering defender and another player in attack to score goals. In recent years teams like Watford, who rely on a long passing game, have resurrected this system with considerable success.

Meanwhile, in Europe, the Italians and Austrians were using a defender behind the back-line who was called a *libero* or 'sweeper'. The Brazilians, however, had won the World Cup in 1958 and 1962 with 4–2–4, having eschewed the sweeper. They still do, preferring to use a back-four of the English style.

By the early Sixties, coaches like Dave Sexton at Chelsea had amended 4–2–4 to 4–3–3 by withdrawing a winger into midfield. Leeds also used this system by withdrawing left-winger Eddie Gray. The 4–2–4 formation had never been a rigid one, as the Hungarians had shown. The wingers would drop back when their side lost the ball, making four men in midfield. Throughout the Sixties and Seventies, the game became more defensive, with fewer attackers and more midfield players.

England's winning of the World Cup in 1966, with Alf Ramsey in charge, was another turning point in the game's evolution. Ramsey initially selected three right-wingers – Terry Paine, John Connelly and Ian Callaghan – and though each played a game in the World Cup, Ramsey did not think any of them was effective enough. By the quarter-final game against Argentina, he had settled on a new 'wingless' formation with Alan Ball and Martin Peters coming into midfield alongside Bobby Charlton and Nobby Stiles. That left just Roger Hunt and Geoff Hurst as attackers.

Once again the rest of football followed a winning formula. Wingers were out. In their place came strength through controlling the midfield. That is still the case today. Good teams will insist on dominating the midfield area. In the 1986 World Cup, teams like Denmark, the USSR and even the winners Argentina, on occasions, used five men in midfield with only one attacker. The idea was to create space with midfield players flooding into it after the ball, making it difficult for opponents to mark them.

There were variations of 4–4–2. Coventry's Gordon Milne used only three defenders, pushing one full-back forward to make four players in midfield and three in attack. That made sense because with other teams using 4–2–4, there was less reason to have four defenders marking two opponents. John Toshack took Swansea to the First Division using three defenders and a sweeper.

The future of team formations

In recent years teams have adapted their tactics according to the requirements of a particular game. No longer do they all play the same way, as happened in the days of WM. Liverpool, for example, will sometimes use a sweeper or three players at the back. They also used Ian Rush as a lone striker with five men in midfield.

What it means is that there is no set way to play the game. The responsibility of coaches is to find out new ways of outwitting their opposite numbers.

Another influential game was England 0 Holland 2 at Wembley in 1977. The Dutch introduced the style of playing without a centre-forward. Johan Cruyff, the player who made them into one of the world's top sides in that era, played in a withdrawn position and Jan Peters, a relative newcomer, scored both goals.

The USSR employed similar tactics at Wembley in 1984 when they won by the same scoreline. They had two strikers playing wide and England were unable to counter them effectively.

Attacking Plays

Successful attack is all about outwitting defenders and that demands movement, intelligent running and good timing. Not all good football is instinctive. Many sound attacking ploys have to be worked out in advance, not to such precision as moves in American football but enough for players to know where they should be in relation to colleagues at certain times.

Teams with a large number of alternative plays will score more goals than those with only one or two plays. Simple tactics involving two or three players can be practised regularly until they are mastered. The game is better if played in pairs with two players working off each other. There are five pairs in each team, discounting the goalkeeper. So the pairs that win their battles with the rival pairs will play a big part in deciding the outcome of the game.

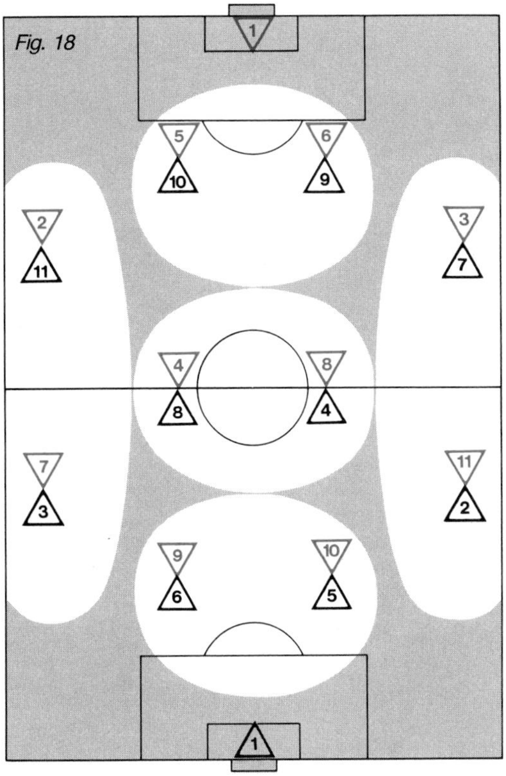

The Overlap

Overlapping full-backs have been a feature of the English game since the early Sixties, when Jimmy Armfield and George Cohen used to make runs in the English side. The essential points are:

1 The timing of the run, so that the full-back does not run into an offside position.

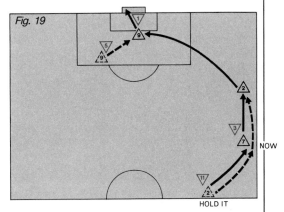

Fig. 18 Working in pairs in a 4.2.4 system
In English football most teams play either a 4.2.4 (see illustration) or a 4.4.2 system. These systems involve five 2 v. 2 areas of the pitch. The team which controls and wins each area is most likely to win the game.

Fig. 19 The overlap
The right-back △ passes to the outside-right △ and shouts 'Hold it!' He then makes his overlapping run wide and behind △. When he gets level with △ he shouts 'Now!' This tells △ to pass the ball down the wing for △ to run onto and cross.

49

2 Intelligent appreciation of making space.

3 Good calling. The full-back will give the ball and shout 'Hold it!' until he is ready to receive a return pass. He will shout 'Now!' when he is passing his colleague.

4 The ball should be played ahead of him, not to his feet or far enough behind his run to slow him down. This will give the full-back time for a split-second glance into the middle to see the passing options.

5 The full-back should be able to cross the ball to the near or far post with accuracy.

The Underlap

The underlap is the overlap inside out. Instead of going on the outside and down the line, the full-back goes on the inside of the winger. It is just as effective as the overlap and the objectives are the same. England full-backs Viv Anderson and Kenny Sansom are very successful with this tactic.

Making space for the centre-back to go forward

No coach likes to see his back-four players not taking part in attacking moves. He wants them to seize every advantage from making positive runs from the back.

Blindside Runs by Midfield Players

This is a simple tactic but an effective one. The run is made across and behind a defender, with a colleague playing the ball in behind the defender. The Italians and Spaniards are particularly skilful at this form of running, called 'blindside running' because the defender will be watching the player with the ball in front of him.

Bryan and Stewart Robson are leading exponents of it in the English game and others good at it were Trevor Brooking and Paul Bracewell.

Fig. 20 The underlap
The right-back △ passes to the outside-right △, then makes his run down the wing, inside ▽. The △ passes the ball down the wing outside ▽ for △ to run onto.

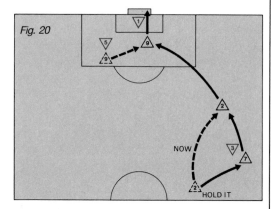

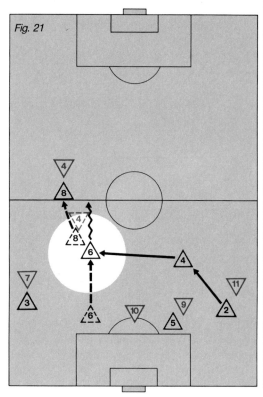

Fig. 21 Making space for the centre-back to go forward
When the back-four have possession, midfield players must vacate their space to make room for the centre-back to get out. In this example the left midfield player ▲ takes the opponent ▽ away, leaving space for ▲ to move out, receive a pass from ▲ and dribble forward with the ball.

Fig. 22 Two examples of blindside runs from midfield
The blindside run is to attack the space behind the opponents' full-backs. Usually it is a midfield player's run but all players should read and appreciate the move.

Fig. 23 Midfield attacking – up-back and through
The ball is played by a midfield player ▲ to a front player ▲. ▲ keeps running. ▲ knocks the ball back to another midfield player ▲ who, in turn, plays a through-ball into space for ▲ to run onto.
A good example of this play ended with a goal scored by Ian Rush in the 1987 Littlewoods Cup Final. The move went McMahon, Rush, Molby, McMahon, and Rush finished it off.

Fig. 24 Midfield attacking – third man running
▲ sets up the move by playing and getting back a short pass off ▲. As the ball comes back, ▲ makes his run; also ▲ makes a run back across the pitch to take a defender ▽ with him. The through-ball from ▲ then goes into space for the third man ▲ to run onto.

Fig. 22

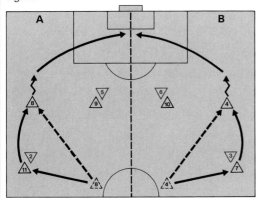

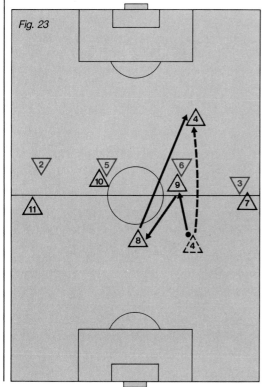

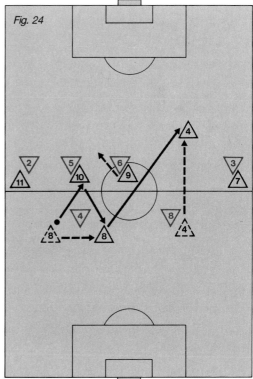

Principles of attacking play

1 *Running off the ball*

From full-backs overlapping to forwards making angled runs, running off the ball is the most effective attacking ploy that can be used. For all but a few minutes of a game, a player will not be in possession, so it is important how he spends that time running to reach a pass, supporting the man in possession or making an unselfish run to take a defender away.

When playing five- or six-a-side training matches, many First Division coaches will impose the following condition: 'When you give it, you go.' In other words, pass and take up a new position. They do it just to get their players into the habit of playing and running off the ball.

2 *The timing of the run*

The intelligent, understanding player times his run. He does not allow himself to be picked up or caught offside. He looks for signals. A midfield player waits until the ball is being knocked back by a front player, then he makes his run. A front player holds his run and waits for the ball to be played before he sets off, or he runs square, waiting for the ball to be passed through.

3 *How to get free from man-for-man marking*

There is only one effective method of getting clear from tight marking – to move in the opposite direction first. The player makes one run for the defender and one run for himself. A winger who wants to receive a pass from his full-back goes away from the full-back first, then checks back to get free to take possession of the ball. A forward who is going to run to the right, moves to the left for a couple of strides which disturbs the defender's balance, and then moves off to the right. A forward who is going to the near post to meet a cross, pulls away first towards the far post to make space for himself, and then makes his run, in to the near post.

4 *Get the cross in*

Crosses are the best providers of goal chances. Flank players who can cross to the near or far post accurately will get more 'assists' than any other player.

5 *Instinctive positioning*

Being in the right place at the right time inside the penalty-area is not an art that can be taught. If it could be, Jimmy Greaves and Denis Law would be the best coaches in the world. Of today's players, Gary Lineker is closest to Greaves in having this 'sixth sense'.

6 *Dribbling*

To have someone in your team who can take on an opponent, and put him out of the game by moving past him with the ball, is also invaluable. Maradona and Laudrup showed how effective dribbling can be in the Mexico World Cup. There is no system of play that can stop top-class dribbling.

The Flat Run

Often it is necessary for the forward to check his forward run to avoid being offside. He then goes off on a flat run – in other words, runs across the pitch parallel to the half-way line. The forward should always remember that his running should be varied so it becomes harder for the defender to go with him.

Rotating

'Rotating' is moving players around to make space. It means defenders interchanging with attackers, and is designed to confuse the opposition.

Rotating is particularly effective against man-for-man marking. Arsenal beat Juventus in a semi-final of the European Cup Winners' Cup in 1980 by exploiting this idea. Their left-back John Devine constantly switched positions with Graham Rix down the left, taking their respective markers into positions where they were uncomfortable.

The purpose of players rotating is to pull their opponents around and make holes in their defensive formation. When central midfield players join in, it becomes even more difficult for the other team to tie down effective man-for-man marking.

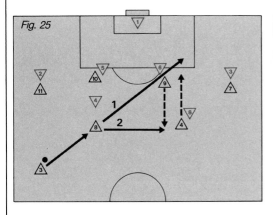

Fig. 25 Rotation – midfield and forwards
While the left midfield player ▲ receives the ball, ▲ and ▲ change position in order to free themselves from markers. ▲ then passes the ball to either of the free team-mates.

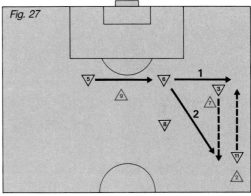

Fig. 27 Rotation in defence – full-back and winger
In order to confuse their opponents and free themselves from markers, ▽ and ▽ rotate. The centre-back ▽ passes to the player who succeeds in getting free.

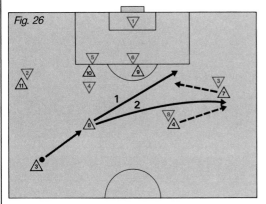

Fig. 26 Rotation – midfield and wingers
While ▲ receives the ball, the wingers ▲ and ▲ change position. ▲ passes the ball to the free player.

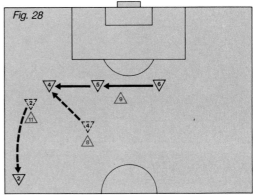

Fig. 28 Rotation in defence – full-back and midfield
The right-back ▽ comes forward and leaves space for the right midfield player ▽ to drop back and receive a pass from the centre-back ▽.

Overs

During the 1970 World Cup, the Brazilians perfected a simple idea which gave them a number of shooting opportunities. Pelé and Tostao were its architects and it was later introduced into English football by Terry Venables when he was manager of QPR.

A midfield player is called upon to serve the ball to the first striker on his side of the pitch who lets it run through his legs when he has heard the call of 'Over!' behind him from a fellow striker. The first striker then spins on a run to his right and the second striker takes possession of the ball. The second striker passes the ball to the first who is now in a clear position. If it comes off, it is a clever move.

Passes Behind Defenders

Strikers are like thieves. They have to be cunning and stealthy to take advantage of those who are trying to stop them. The outstanding strikers like Jimmy Greaves, Denis Law and, from today's game, Ian Rush have the necessary instinct to time their runs behind defenders and not end up being called back for offside. It has to be instinct to be in the right position at the right time, otherwise they would have become coaches themselves and passed their skills on to thousands of others. Because it is not a gift that can be handed on, few players have it and fewer still are capable of talking about how they do it.

Rush scored against Everton in the 1986

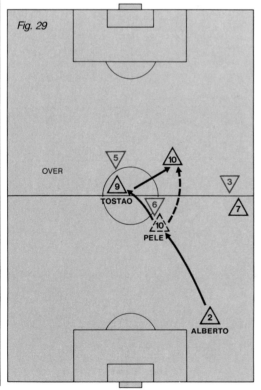

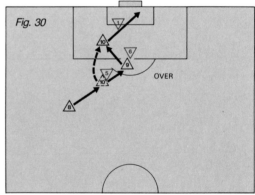

Fig. 29 Overs
The Brazilians used this play very successfully in the World Cup in Mexico, 1970. The ball was passed up to Pele △ by Carlos Alberto △. Tostao △ shouted 'Over!' Pele let the ball run through his legs and then spun round and ran into the space behind the opponents ▽ and ▽.

Fig. 30 Overs on the edge of the box
Overs are most effective on the edge of the opponents' box. △ Passes the ball to △. △ shouts 'Over!' and △ lets it run through his legs to △. △ spins round and behind the defenders ▽ and ▽ to receive the return pass and try for a shot at goal.

FA Cup Final with a move that was typical of him. Jan Molby played a pass behind the Everton defence and Rush was on to it.

Rush's colleagues in Italy took a long time to discover that he prefers the ball being played into space, not to his feet. He points to where he wants it and usually has the pace and anticipation to get to the ball before any defender or the goalkeeper.

Forwards making space

Making space for himself is a vital part of the forward's armoury. Forwards must never remain static or make straight runs. They must aim to move off in one direction and dart back into another to receive the ball.

Forwards getting free from marking

Fig. 31 The forward △ is marked by the opponents' centre-back ▽. To make space to receive a pass from the right-back △, △ pulls forwards, threatening ▽'s back. When △ looks up he comes back into the space to receive the ball.

Fig. 32 Here the forward △ works in the opposite way. He comes back towards the full-back △, pulling his marker ▽ forward. When the full-back looks up, △ spins into the space down the wing.

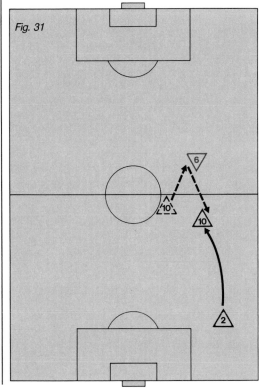

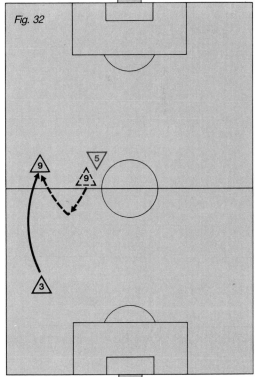

To make space for yourself you must move in the opposite direction first. In other words:
One run for the defender.
One run for yourself.

Fig. 33 The forward ▲ makes a short run. His marker ▽ goes with him. When ▲ looks up, ▲ spins back into the space, looking for a diagonal pass from him.

Fig. 34 Here the forward ▲ works in the opposite way. He moves away to the back of the marker ▽. When ▲ lifts his head, ▲ makes a diagonal run for a through-ball behind the defence.

Fig. 35 The 'Gary Lineker'
Lineker ▲ moves as though he is going to run wide, taking his marker ▽ with him. He then spins back inside the marker for a pass in the space behind the defence.

Fig. 36 Two examples of how a winger can get free from marking
A When the left-back ▲ receives the ball, the outside-left ▲ comes deep towards the ball then spins for a pass inside the right-back ▽
B When the right-back ▲ receives the ball, the right-winger ▲ moves away from the ball (about 10 yards), taking his marker ▽ with him. ▲ then spins back to receive the ball to feet.

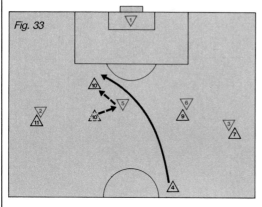

Fig. 33

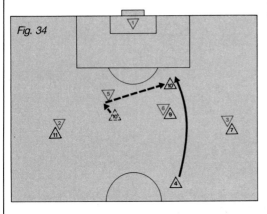

Fig. 34

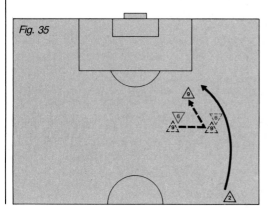

Fig. 35

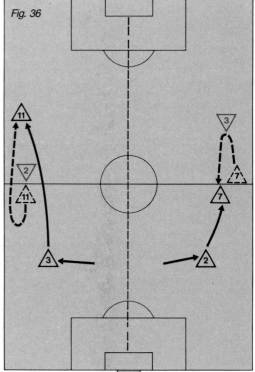

Fig. 36

Running with the Ball

Running with the ball is not an art which is seen too often in the English game. This is because defenders tend to 'squeeze' the play into a narrow strip as far away as possible from their own goal. There is much less space for players to control the ball and run into. But in the Mexico World Cup, which was notable for the way in which teams with sweepers allowed play to be stretched out (the reverse of what happens in the Football League), there were countless examples of outstanding running with the ball.

(*Below*) England centre-half Mark Wright has good control for a defender and often brings the ball out of defence with strong runs. Here his head is up and he is looking towards the next challenge after leaving the West German Lothar Matthaus behind. The ball is at the right distance from his foot, about four or five feet – he is in full control of the situation.

> **Good football is 'G' force –
> GET IT!
> GIVE IT!
> GO!**

It is perhaps understandable that the best runners with the ball in the English game are nearly all foreigners – Ossie Ardiles when he was in his prime at Tottenham, Frans Thijssen when he was at Ipswich and the Manchester United pair Jesper Olsen and John Sivebaek.

There are a number of points to be observed when running with the ball:

1 If there is space to run into, move as quickly as possible. Then, having killed the space, run at an opponent, commit him, then use the ball.

2 Do not have too many touches. If the player does, it will slow him down. If he is going twenty yards and the route is clear, two or three touches are preferable to four or five. But the ball should not be too far ahead. He may have to check and change direction or use a pass quickly.

3 The touches of the ball can be with the inside or outside of the foot, or even the toe, whatever is convenient and will not disrupt the stride.

4 The eyes should be directed forwards, not downwards at the ball. If the player touches the ball often, it means he is looking down instead of up as he should be.

5 If there are defenders in the way at the end of the run, the player can eliminate them by making a change of direction to send them the wrong way. The momentum of the run will carry him past them. The quicker the movement, the less chance they have of winning the ball. The object must be to commit the defender and beat him.

Running off the Ball

Ron Greenwood used to say that running off the ball was the most important part of the game. On average, a player is in possession for only two or three minutes. Most of the game he is playing without the ball, so it makes sense to suggest that considerable attention should be given to this part of football.

The intelligent player will always be looking for space. He will be out to support the player on the ball, giving him a passing alternative. He will be making all kinds of runs, not just the obvious one, until he gets the ball. When he gets it, his aim should be to use it profitably and then start up the process all over again. Support play requires an unselfish attitude and demands a high level of fitness.

Good teams are full of outstanding support players, and in the past twenty years Liverpool and Spurs have been the best examples. At any time in a match a Liverpool player knows there will always be someone within range who is available to receive the ball.

The bad teams are those with players who wait for the ball to come to them. Good teams are full of movement.

Turning on the Edge of the Box

As a variation to laying the ball off to a colleague, the striker can turn on it and try to create a scoring chance on his own, especially if the play is pressed up against the edge of the penalty-area. The defenders will be in a line to avoid putting an opponent onside and there will be no cover behind them if he succeeds.

It is important that the ball is played accurately and firmly to his feet. The receiver can drag the ball back with the inside of his right foot, pivoting on his left foot and aiming to send the defender the wrong way with a slight movement of his shoulder. All the forward needs is enough space to get a shot in. He does not have to be completely clear.

An alternative is to take the ball with the outside of the foot, first moving to the left and then turning back. Once more the forward only needs half a yard to get a shot in but with this turn it will be with his left foot.

(*Below*) Kenny Dalglish was a master at receiving the ball and turning with it. Here he is opposed by Manchester United and England captain Bryan Robson. Dalglish is perfectly balanced with arms outstretched and eyes on the ball.

Diagonal Play (The Rush Factor)

The geometry of forward passes and forward runs fits together like this:

Forward run–Diagonal pass

Forward pass–Diagonal run

It depends mainly on the types of tactical defence you are playing against.

The logic of diagonal play

The 'Gary Lineker' runs

Fig. 37 The right midfield player △ passes a straight ball into the path of the striker ⚑ 's diagonal run.

Fig. 38 The right midfield player △ passes a diagonal ball into the path of the striker ⚑ 's straight run.

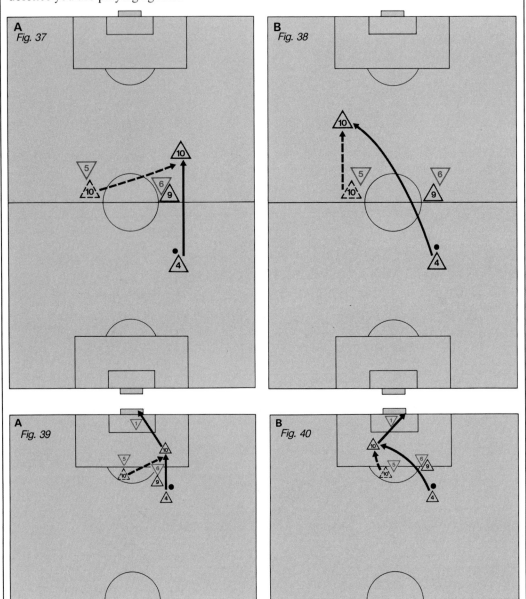

A Fig. 37

B Fig. 38

A Fig. 39

B Fig. 40

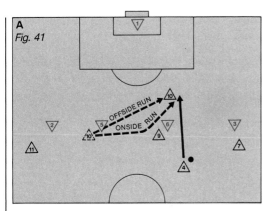

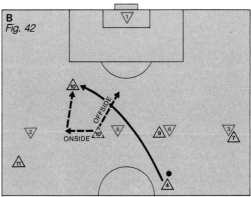

The 'Ian Rush' runs
Fig. 39 Straight pass — diagonal run. A well-timed and delicate pass on the edge of the opponents' box.

Fig. 40 Diagonal pass — straight run, on the edge of the opponents' box.

(*Below*) In his Liverpool days, Ian Rush gets away from Juventus defenders Sergio Brio and Marco Tardelli. He already has his next move worked out as he frees himself from their attentions.

Beating a zonal defence

Flat runs
Fig. 41 The striker ⚠ flattens his diagonal run, keeping onside and waiting for the midfield player ⚠ to play his pass through the zonal defence.

Fig. 42 The striker ⚠ pulls back away from his marker ⚠, looking across the defenders to keep onside, and making space for a diagonal pass from ⚠.

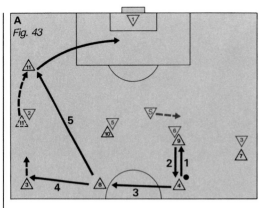

A

Fig. 43

Getting free from marking and playing against the sweeper

It is essential that strikers work together in training on ideas about how to lose defenders and make space for each other on crosses.

Movement in the box is vital. A good forward is not only aware of the space for himself, but is also aware of making space for team-mates.

One of the forwards needs to make life difficult for the sweeper by keeping very close and making plenty of runs to pull him out of position.

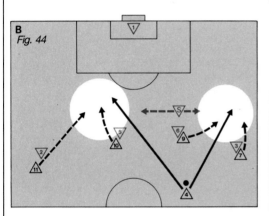

B

Fig. 44

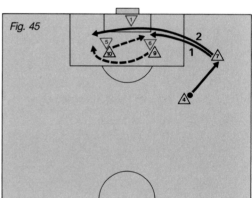

Fig. 45

Beating the sweeper

Fig. 43 This is an example of changing the play to beat the sweeper. The right midfield player △ passes up to the striker △. This pulls the sweeper ▽ over to cover. △ then receives a return-pass and changes the play with a pass to △. △ has two choices of pass: either (4) to the left-back △ who can attack, or (5) to the outside-left △ who can get a cross in early.

Fig. 44 Straight passes against the sweeper ▽ are futile. The passes need to be diagonal into the areas the sweeper cannot cover. The forwards △, △, △ and △ must make runs to exploit those areas.

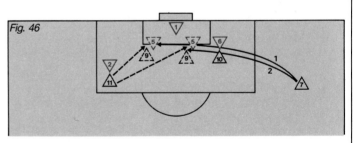

Fig. 46

Strikers getting free from markers in the penalty box

Fig. 45 Strikers △ and △ work together to get free from marking. As the ball is passed to the outside-right △, △ spins away to the far post, leaving room at the near post for the △ to run into. △ can either pass (1) to △ on the near post, or (2) to △ on the far post.

Fig. 46 △ is crossing the ball. If the centre-forward △ is central, the winger △ gets into the far post; but if △ pulls to the far post, △ gets into the centre of goal.

The Target Man

The striker who is capable of knocking the ball back to a colleague is known as the 'target man' in English football. He uses himself as a set-up player, accepting and controlling passes under pressure from a defender behind him. But he does not always have to lay the ball off the first time. He can seek to control it before releasing it to a supporting player. John Radford and Ray Kennedy were superb target men at Arsenal, enabling the defenders to find them with long passes which turned defence into attack. The target man is still in style but these days there are fewer of them.

(*Below*) In his heyday, Ray Kennedy of Arsenal and Liverpool was one of the best target men in British football.

Because of the shortage, most teams make do with a target man and a striker who plays off him. It is rare to find a team with two out-and-out target men.

Modern strikers tend to be quicker and smaller in the Tony Cottee/Frank McAvennie mould. Yet the Football League has probably produced more good target players than any comparable League, players like John Toshack and Kevin Keegan when they played together at Liverpool, Gary Lineker and Graeme Sharp at Everton, and Frank Stapleton and Alan Sunderland at Arsenal.

Understanding between the defender making the long pass and the striker has to be good for the move to be effective. The striker must not attempt to get away from his marker until he sees that his colleague is ready to pass. When the defender lifts his head to see where the ball is coming from,

that is the time for the striker to make his move.

The striker must come off at an angle. The reasons for this are threefold. Firstly, it means the striker is giving less ground away because he is not running back too far towards his team-mate. Secondly, it stops the centre-half getting in front of him and getting to the ball first. And thirdly, it makes it easier for him to turn when he receives the ball.

Hitting the target man

Fig. 47 English football is about hitting the target man early. The target man ⚠ comes off at an angle. Note the supporting 'knock-back' positions of ⚠ and ⚠.

Fig. 48 The target man ⚠ comes back into the space for the knock-back. ⚠ makes room by running wide. Note the supporting positions of ⚠ and ⚠.

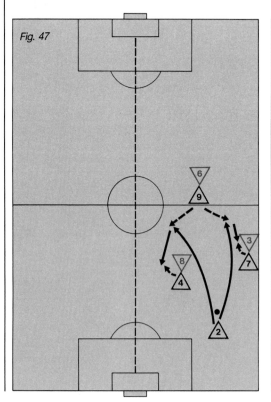

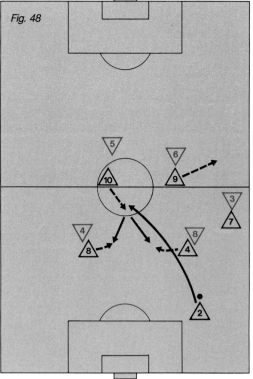

The ball can be played short to feet or even bounced in front of him. Some of the best exponents of this type of pass were Bobby Moore, the former West Ham and England defender, George Burley, the ex-Ipswich and Sunderland right-back and Phil Neal, formerly of Northampton, Liverpool and England.

When the ball is on its way, the receiver must have a picture in his mind of the position of his colleagues around him. He can then pick out one to whom he can play the ball off, and that requires a deft touch.

A player who will let the ball rebound off him in an uncontrolled manner is a liability.

Playing the ball down the channels

An alternative is for the defender to play the ball over a full-back. Similar principles are required but the forward also has the chance of directing the ball towards goal and getting a shot in. First he must seek to escape his marker by moving one way and then going in the other direction.

Dribbling

Players who can dribble and beat opponents are match winners. They can beat any defensive system or any tactic. Unfortunately, there are not many great dribblers in the world game.

Wiel Coerver, the Dutch coach who specialises in teaching dribbling skills, has written a book about the subject and says that players can be taught a variety of tricks to enable them to master the art. I would not disagree with him. It *is* possible to coach dribbling skills. But in the main most players learn from watching top-class players on television, or at matches.

Stanley Matthews, for example, almost invariably went the same way. He would feint to his left and go past his opponent on the right. Defenders knew what to expect, but his ability to read when his opponent was off balance, and his control of the ball, change of direction and acceleration were such that few of them were able to catch him.

Many qualities are essential to dribbling, including pace, strength, stamina and determination, but balance is vital. All the great players have had it, from Tom Finney and Stanley Matthews to George Best and Diego Maradona. It enables them to ride tackles and still get through. It enables them to evade unfair challenges, to retain possession when the odds are against them.

Maradona is brilliant at holding off challenges. He will use any part of his

(*Below*) Diego Maradona, the world's best dribbler, on his way past Peter Reid and Terry Fenwick in Mexico. Notice that the ball is within a comfortable distance to enable him to keep running at speed.

(*Right*) Maradona shows his strength and single-mindedness as he scores Argentina's second goal against England despite the challenges of Terry Butcher and Peter Shilton.

anatomy – his hips, his shoulders, his buttocks or his arms – to ward off defenders. And he does it at pace. He is amazingly quick for a player of his stocky build. Such is his balance and strength that if he is on a run and is impeded, he bounces up like a rubber duck righting itself in the bath! He has a low centre of gravity, and that helps. Most dribblers go wide down the flanks but Maradona will often try to get through down the middle.

The object of the dribbler will be to set the defender up, get him off balance, unsettle him and then leave him behind. Maradona does that better than anyone and, unlike most of those who try to emulate him, he does not have one basic trick. He is master of the art of changing direction, with the instep, outside of the foot, or sole of the foot, at pace.

Some players will aim to defeat their opponent by a sudden movement of the body. Chris Waddle does it. John Barnes uses his shoulder, dropping it one way and then moving the other way.

Glenn Roeder developed a technique of putting his right foot over the ball and then taking it to his left with the outside of his left foot. Charlie Cooke, the former Chelsea and Scotland winger, would move the ball between his feet as in a pin-table game, and Pat Nevin, his successor at Stamford Bridge, has similar tricks.

(*Below*) England forward Chris Waddle pushes the ball through the legs of Arsenal skipper Kenny Sansom. It is called the 'nut meg'.

(*Opposite*) Charlie Cooke, one of the outstanding dribblers of British post-war years, in action for Chelsea.

(*Above left*) France's Bruno Bellone in the classic confrontation position as he faces Nikolai Larionov of the USSR. Bellone's balance is good and he is poised to make his move with either foot.

(*Below left*) George Best had an infinite variety of tricks and here he is with Nobby Stiles, one of England's finest tacklers.

The forward wants the defender to commit himself. Once the defender makes the first move, he will beat him.

All the leading dribblers have good acceleration – Matthews, Finney, Best, Gento, Czibor, Garrincha and Maradona. Without it, they can be caught by a defender making a recovery tackle. It is one of the chief requirements. Others are good, tight control of the ball and the ability to change direction speedily. Determination is also needed.

Worming your way through a crowded defence is not an easy, clean-cut business. The dribbler must be brave and be prepared to rough it if necessary.

(Below) *Dribbling – leg over the ball dummy*
As Barnes approaches Adams, he dummies his left leg over the ball as though he is going to the left, then accelerates away to the right.

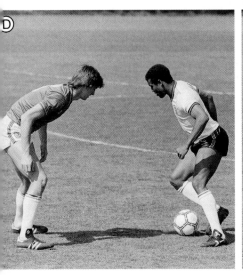

Beating more than one defender

When teams know they are up against a good dribbler, they will cover the defender taking him on, to block his path. If one defender is lined up behind the other, the art of changing direction becomes crucial. The dribbler will be seeking to get them square to him. That way he can put the ball between them and squeeze through. If they both try to tackle him at the same time, they run the risk of fouling.

Crossing

An accurate crosser of the ball is invaluable to his team.

Statistics show that seventy-five per cent or more goals come from wing crosses, so the ability to cross is a very important asset. Most players should be able to cross the ball on the run. The art of making a good cross is to pick out a colleague in a good position and eliminate the goalkeeper. The cross which is too close to the goalkeeper, inside the six-yard box, for example, is a wasted effort.

There are three alternative targets or zones to aim for:

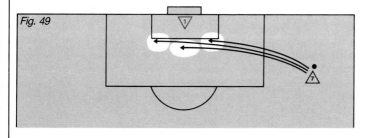

1 The near post, for the flick-on header or first-time shot.

2 The far post for the header back into goal.

3 The centre of goal if there is someone free in that position.

Fig. 49 The three crossing zones
These three areas are the goalkeeper's vulnerable spots. Headed goals come from these areas.

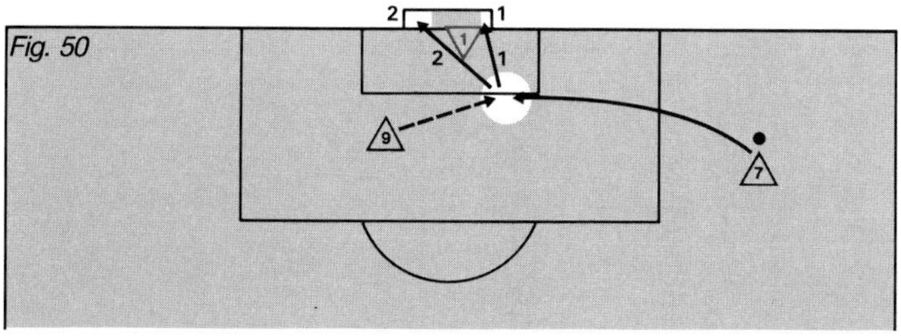

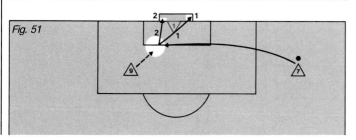

Fig. 50 The near-post cross
This can result in either (1) a power-header into the near-post area, or (2) a glancing flick into the far post.

Fig. 51 The far-post cross
This can result in either (1) a header back across the goalkeeper to the far post, or (2) a low header into the near post.

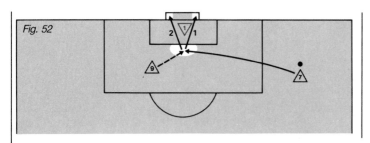

Fig. 52

Fig. 52 Cross into the central area outside the six-yard box
Power and accuracy are essential in this area for headers high or low into the near (1) or far (2) posts.

Most professional clubs spend at least two sessions a week on practising crosses. The chief reason a cross goes out of play is that usually the crosser is facing straight ahead and cannot wrap his foot around the ball to get the right angle.

Few players can cross accurately in that position. George Best and Alan Hinton could, and of today's players Trevor Steven and John Barnes are rare examples of good crossers. Ideally, the player needs to turn infield, facing the goal, to give himself the necessary angle. If he is aiming for the far post, he will kick the ball with the laces.

If he is directing the ball towards the near post, he will use the side of the foot. In each case the motion of the foot coming through the ball will impart spin, causing a slight 'bend' which takes the ball away from goal.

Some wingers think they have to beat the full-back before they cross but that is not always the case. They only need half a yard lead on their opponent to be able to get their cross in.

(Right) Bending the cross in
Notice how the foot imparts spin on the ball with the follow-through, the toe pointing to the byline.

(Below) Getting the cross in
Barnes makes enough room to get his cross in without beating Adams.

Full-backs in the modern game also have to be proficient at crossing. Too often they get into a good overlapping position and waste their opportunity. They need to practise crossing as much as flank players.

Types of Crosses

There are least *six* types of crosses.

Over the last fifteen years the variety in crosses has improved more than any other part of the game. The problems goalkeepers and defenders have to cope with these days keep them continually under pressure.

Years ago there were only two types of crosses – far post or pulled back from the byline. Old films of wingers like Stanley Matthews and Tom Finney will confirm this.

The six used today are:

1 *Near post* – played into the space on the near post at head height and under. The basic technique is to play the cross a little under-weighted, so that the forward can time his run into the space. Forwards who are particularly skilful in this situation are Clive Allen and Adrian Heath.

2 *Far post* – Played high to the far post to eliminate the goalkeeper. It is a cross to get to the back of defenders for the big men to attack. Mark Hateley and Niall Quinn are good examples of those who profit from this type of cross.

3 *Centre goal* – Obviously the cross must be outside the six-yard box, otherwise it would be the goalkeeper's ball. More headers are scored from this position. (Examples: Ian Rush and Luther Blissett.)

4 *Curled in early* – Having got behind the full-back, the player crosses the ball early into the path of incoming forwards. (Examples: Gary Lineker and Ian Rush.)

5 *Inswinging* – Another difficult one to deal with. The far post is the best area for this cross, and the ball should be whipped in. Chris Waddle is outstanding at it.

6 *Hard- and low-driven* – This cross can ricochet anywhere and benefits mainly small forwards though it is effective for any size of player. It is Gary Lineker's speciality because he is so quick in these situations. Other leading exponents of this type of cross are Craig Johnston and Kevin Sheedy.

(Right and below) Crossing to the far post
Notice how Barnes gets around the ball and faces towards goal.

The Early Cross

Having got in behind the full-back, the earlier the player crosses the better. The object must be to get the ball in behind defenders who will be recovering and facing their own goal, risking 'own goals'.

Forwards receiving the ball from this type of cross are in a great position. A side-footer on target is often all that is needed to put the ball into the net.

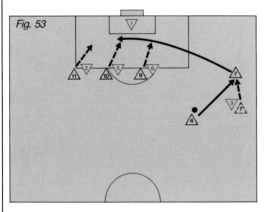

Fig. 53

Fig. 53 The early cross
When there is a break on the wing the ball must be crossed in early behind defenders. The goal is then at the strikers' mercy.

Cutting the ball back

The ball pulled back from the byline into the path of oncoming forwards is the most dangerous pass in the game. Attacking players cannot be offside because they are behind the ball and they do not need more than a touch, a side-foot or power-header to score.

The crosser should look up early, locate his target, either a team-mate or a zone, and then look down again at the ball. But because of the presence of a defender, this is not always possible. Therefore I would say to young players that it is better to keep your eyes on the ball and make sure your

crossing technique is good. Then it will be up to the forward to reach the cross.

The player going for the cross will be aiming to 'pass' the ball into the net. The impetus of the cross will provide the necessary pace. All he has to do is ensure he is on target.

The Inswinging Cross

Instead of seeking to outpace a full-back and cross on the run, a player on the right side of the pitch will sometimes decide to check back inside and cross with his left foot.

Because of the crosser's position and angle to goal, it is easy to put in an inswinging cross. He will aim to swing the ball into the far-post area across the face of the goal and provide a colleague with an opportunity to score.

The same situation applies on the left side of the pitch with the winger checking back on to his right foot.

Escaping a Marker and Converting Crosses with the Head

Getting across and in front of the defender is the crucial factor on crosses. It is where determination comes in. The forward who waits for the ball to reach him never scores or gets headers in.

The forward who wants to score with headers needs to be first to the ball. He has his weight on his front foot, ready to strike, and he has the desire and bravery to take the knocks.

Obviously, marking in the box is a lot tighter than outside the box. A forward must be cunning, brave and time his runs decisively to score. He has to anticipate what kind of cross is coming into the box.

He should also not show his intentions too early. That near-post run must be

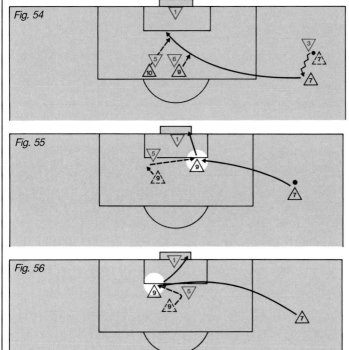

Fig. 54

Fig. 55

Fig. 56

(*Above*) Welsh winger Robbie James crosses on the run as Oxford's Les Phillips tries to block. He has connected with the side of the foot and is leaning back slightly.

Fig. 54 The inswinging cross
If the winger △ cannot get past the full-back ▽ on the outside, he can check inside on to his left foot and cross in an inswinging ball.

Escaping your marker on crosses

Fig. 55 The striker △ pulls behind the defender ▽ as though going to the far post, leaving and making more space on the near post. Making sure his timing is right, he then sprints into the space on the near post. The problem for the defender is that he cannot watch two things at once, the man and the ball.

Fig. 56 The striker △ disguises his intentions by taking a few steps to the near post and then dragging back to the far post.

disguised and timed to perfection. When he and the ball arrive in the same space together, he is in business. Ability takes over. He must ask himself what kind of header is demanded and how to achieve it:

High – He must get his take-off right. He must get the ball on target.

Head-height – Does it require a bullet-like header or a deft glance?

Waist-height – Is it a brave, diving header, with eyes on the ball, directing it on target?

Knee-height – Does it need a glancing volley or a stab inside the near post?

Low – Can he keep it down? It is easy to lean back meaning the ball will fly over the bar.

Shadow practice

Shadow practice was invented in the Sixties by Alan Brown, the former Burnley, Sheffield Wednesday and Sunderland manager.

The simplest way of describing it is 'a practice game without opposition'. The team lines up in its normal formation and advances upfield as it would in a game, except that there are no players to stop them, and finishes the move off with an attempt on goal.

Coaches use shadow practice to get their ideas across. It demands a good application, attitude and imagination.

There are three basic ways of doing it:

1 The goalkeeper starts the practice by either throwing or kicking the ball out. The coach will ask for a certain aspect to be included in the attack – an overlap, a near-post cross or anything he thinks needs practising.

2 The ten outfield players attack the goalkeeper who is in the opposite goal. The goalkeeper starts the practice by kicking long and high downfield. The defence get the ball under control and start their attack. Once more the coach asks for a tactical innovation from the team.

3 When the ball is being passed about, the coach blows his whistle which is the signal for the midfield players to turn and attack the back-four. The coach will be looking for certain aspects of attacking or defending to be brought out.

Shooting

Opinions are divided among coaches about whether it is better to be deliberate and place the ball or get in an early shot which has pace. Jimmy Greaves and Kenny Dalglish represented the first school of thought. Many of their goals were stroked, almost passed, into the corner of the net where goalkeepers find it hardest to protect their goal. They were rarely off target. Bobby Charlton and Malcolm Macdonald personified what power-shooting was all about. They would direct shots at the full target, not picking an exact spot, from ranges of up to thirty yards or more.

I would not disagree with either theory. It must be up to the individual player. If he has the temperament which enables him to look up and take aim before placing his shot, then he will be well-advised to rely on accuracy. Other players like Charlton, Macdonald and also Geoff Hurst, powerfully-built players, found it more profitable to strike the ball hard at the full target.

What I do not like to see is players 'snatching' at the ball and being over-anxious. Shooting requires a certain temperament. Frenzied players rarely make consistent goalscorers. Good coaches will put forwards in shooting situations as often as possible in training so they get used to the amount of time they have and what kind of shot is needed.

The art of training goalscorers is to strike a balance between good shooting practices and instinctive ability. The inherent ability of a striker is being in the right place at the right time and getting his shot on target. If the coach spends too much time asking the player to analyse what he is doing, the player can lose his instinctive ability to score. It is dangerous to talk about aiming for perfection.

Many goals are tap-ins or toe-pokes around the six-yard area. Gary Lineker scores many of his goals in this way. They are not the result of either calmly-placed shots or powerful blasts. Sometimes they come from a different part of the player's anatomy, his knee or thigh. They happen because the forward is reacting more quickly than the nearest defender.

Shooting on the Half-Volley

A similar technique is required to that of ordinary shooting, with the head steady, non-kicking foot alongside the ball, arms outstretched and a high backlift. Timing is important, with the ball being struck as it hits the ground. It is absolutely vital to get right over the ball. Concentrate, especially if under pressure, and keep it down by keeping the toe down. If that does not happen, the ball will sail over the crossbar.

When the ball is dropping towards the ground, the player does not often have much time. He might well be under pressure from an opponent, and the ball may be on his 'wrong foot'. In order to avoid this problem, it is essential that he uses both feet when practising.

Volleying the Ball from the Side

The non-kicking foot will be the base for balance and pivoting, enabling the kicking foot to come up high, almost parallel to the

ground, as it strikes the top or the middle of the ball.

Keeping the volley down is vital. No goalkeeper likes to deal with a shot that bounces as it approaches him.

I always say to forwards, 'Don't be afraid to fail.' I tell them it is better to try and fail, than not try at all. It does not matter if they keep missing the target. With practice they will eventually succeed. But no coach will be happy if players shun shooting opportunities. Players do this through lack of confidence but they can only regain confidence if they keep trying and succeed.

(*Far left*) Former Ipswich striker Alan Brazil volleys the ball from the side past Sunderland defender Rob Hindmarch.

(*Above*) *Face-on volley*
Eyes on the ball, toe down, contact with laces.

Power Shooting from the Edge of the Box

Before shooting, it is important to glance up to see where the goalkeeper is, but when the foot starts coming through, the head has to be down and the eyes firmly on the ball. Other points are:

1 The non-kicking foot is alongside the ball.

2 The higher the backlift, the more power, although a player like Charlie George could achieve great power with a short backlift.

3 Arms are outstretched to the side to help balance.

4 The toe of the kicking foot is kept down and the contact is made in the centre of the ball with the laces.

5 When striking the ball, the non-kicking foot leaves the ground.

If the head is right over the ball, it is easier to keep the shot down. A low shot, particularly when it is aimed at the corner of the goal, is harder to stop than a high shot, unless the high shot is directed inside the angle of the crossbar and the post.

I recommend tying a rope four feet high between the posts at shooting practices and asking the players to shoot under the rope.

(Overleaf) Side-on volley
Barnes drops his right shoulder so that he can get his left foot high over the ball, keeping it down.

Shooting from an Angle

When a forward is approaching goal on an angle, I recommend shooting hard and low inside the far post. The reasons why the far post is preferred are:

1 If the goalkeeper makes a save, the likelihood is that he will push the ball out into the path of oncoming forwards.

2 If the ball hits the far post, it is likely to come back into play.

Fig. 57

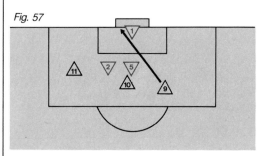

3 If the shot is not on target and is pulled across goal, a supporting player running in on the far post can reach it. Many goals are scored in this way.

There are two other methods of shooting from an angle. The first is the bending shot inside the far post (*Fig. 58*). Struck properly with the inside of the foot, it will elude the goalkeeper and enter the goal under the angle of the bar and post which is a difficult place for the goalkeeper to protect. The natural curve of the shot will take the ball away from the goalkeeper, who will have narrowed the angle, and back on to the target. Both Kenny Dalglish and Clive Allen have been adept at this type of shot.

The second is the angled chip (*Fig. 59*). The forward will judge the position of the goalkeeper off his line as he closes the angle down and chip the ball high enough to clear his upstretched arms, so that it ends up in the net inside the far post.

Fig. 57 Shooting from an angle
A hard low shot by ⚠ inside the far post is difficult for the goalkeeper to save. If the goalkeeper does manage to palm the ball out, ⚠ or ⚠ can take advantage of the knock-down. If the ball hits the post it will also rebound towards ⚠ and ⚠ .
If ⚠ drags the shot and misses, ⚠ could move in for a shot at goal.

Fig. 58

Fig. 59

From positions outside the box, even the power shot may prove inadequate to beat a good goalkeeper. The intelligent player will make up his mind about what to do when he looks at where the goalkeeper is standing. Most goalkeepers will come off their line to narrow the angle when a player is shaping to shoot from that range. By doing so, they make themselves vulnerable to the bending shot struck with the side of the foot, or the chip, jabbing the toe under the ball for a sharp trajectory. Glenn Hoddle is perhaps the leading exponent of this type of shot.

The Forward Against the Goalkeeper, One to One

There will be occasions in a match when a forward breaks through and finds himself with only the goalkeeper to beat. Scoring looks a formality, but it is not. The better

the goalkeeper, the more difficult the task of the forward.

The goalkeeper will come off his line to narrow the angle and give his opponent as little of his goal to look at as possible. An ordinary goalkeeper will keep coming and will try and dive into the line of the shot. But a good goalkeeper will hold his position, forcing the forward to make his move.

What happens next depends on the forward's personal preference. Malcolm Macdonald nearly always shot hard and low, close to the side of the goalkeeper's feet. He claimed that a shot of that type was very hard to stop and he was right.

Other players elect to get the 'keeper to commit himself and chip the ball over his dive or, if the ball is bouncing, volley it over his head. Neither task is easy when a player is running hard at goal. It demands a lot of practice to perfect these techniques.

It will help if the forward can disguise his

intentions. He can pretend to shoot but take the ball on instead, committing the goalkeeper to his dive. A good goalkeeper, however, might make a dummy of his own, forcing the forward to go the side he wants him to go.

If the forward decides to dribble round the goalkeeper, he must make sure he puts the ball far enough to the side of the goalkeeper to stop him reaching it. And he must also ensure that he does not knock it too far past him, so that it goes out of play or leaves him with a bad angle. Going too wide gives defenders a chance to get back and clear the ball off the line.

The forward has to be positive and know what he wants to do. He must be confident about his intentions.

When to Shoot and When Not to Shoot

When players get into quality football, it is important that they know when to shoot for goal and when to pull the ball across the goal to a better-placed team-mate.

The instinctive goalscorers have a 'sixth sense' which tells them when they are in the right place at the right time.

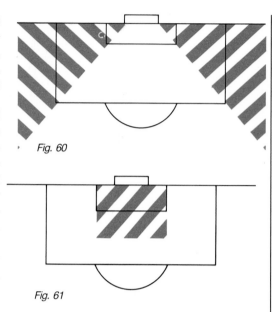

Fig. 60

Fig. 61

When to shoot and when not to shoot

Fig. 60 By drawing a line from the post to the corner of the penalty box on both sides of the goal, we can get a good idea of the best area for scoring goals. Outside the lines – pull the ball across goal for team-mates. Inside the lines – go for your shot.

Fig. 61 Another way of looking at things. Ninety per cent of all goals scored come from an imaginary second six-yard box area. By drawing this other six-yard box, we can see the area to be in to score goals consistently.

Defending

Defending as a Team in Midfield

The players at the back are not the only players whose job it is to defend. Once the ball is lost, it is the duty of all ten outfield players to try and win it back by defending intelligently.

The art of defending in midfield is to prevent opponents from playing the ball forward. If they can be forced to play the ball square, there is more chance of making an interception. And the more square passes they can be persuaded to make, the greater the chance of a breakdown or interception.

It is difficult to win the ball in midfield by straightforward one-against-one tackling. The way the game is played in England, the team that wins the majority of the knock-downs controls the game.

When a move breaks down, the midfield players must track back and pick up opponents. It is a task that requires stamina and endurance plus organisation. But there are times when a midfield player can save his legs by 'handing over' his opponent to a zonal marker behind him.

In an ideal midfield quartet, one player in central midfield will be a good attacking player and his partner a good defensive player, with two wide players who can both attack and defend. One of the four will have the responsibility of allocating marking responsibilities.

Man-for-man marking

The defending player will sometimes be given the task of doing a man-for-man job almost to the exclusion of anything else. Lothar Matthaus was given this task in the West Germany v. Argentina match in Mexico and his mission was to stop Diego Maradona. It is an unselfish role but an invaluable one.

Midfield defending systems

There are four generally-used systems of midfield defensive play:

1 The English four-in-a-row.

2 The Ipswich 'diamond' system, with one of the midfield players withdrawn into an anchor role in front of the back-four and another player pushed forward in front of him and behind the strikers.

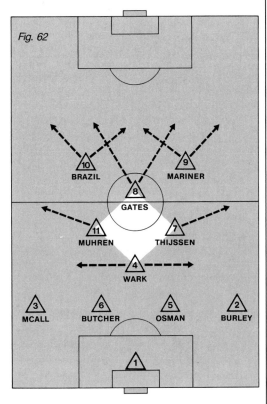

Fig. 62 Midfield defending systems
The Ipswich 'diamond'.

3 The Continental trio, with the centre man holding in front of the defenders and allowing the players alongside him to go forward.

4 The five-man midfield used by the USSR, Belgium, Tottenham and, in their European Cup days, Nottingham Forest. One of the central players will 'hold', with the others breaking forward to help the single striker. One of the five will be used in a more advanced position behind the striker.

Defending as a Team – Back Four Systems

Zonal system

There are two basic systems used in defending – zonal and the sweeper system. The first system, zonal, is commonly used in the English Football League and involves four back players in a line. Each man will hold his position and pick up whoever comes into his zone. If the man he is marking moves to other zones, he will pass him on to a colleague.

If the attack comes down the right, for example, the back-four will pull over in that direction like a tow bar pulling a broken-down car. Each defender covers the other and the left side of the pitch will be less protected.

Should the opponents attack down the middle, the full-backs tuck in, forming an apex or pyramid formation which forces the opposition to play the ball into wide, less dangerous positions. The essentials of the system are to mark and cover and not be pulled out of position. It is a system for good, intelligent back-four players, sound technicians who can send opponents up blind alleys and make defending look easy. Liverpool provide us with an outstanding example of how it should be done.

There has to be a lot of talking among the defenders to make sure the system works.

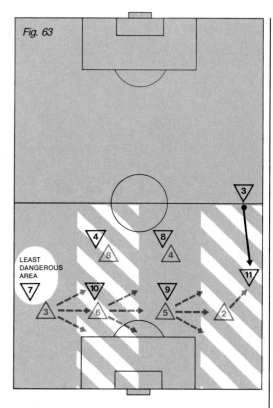

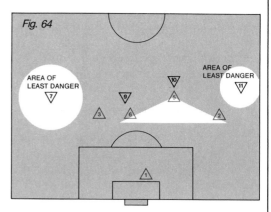

Zonal defence

Fig. 63 The back-four hold their zones and pick up any opponent who comes into these. They also cover the blind side of fellow defenders.

Fig. 64 The pyramid zonal cover forces the play into wide positions.

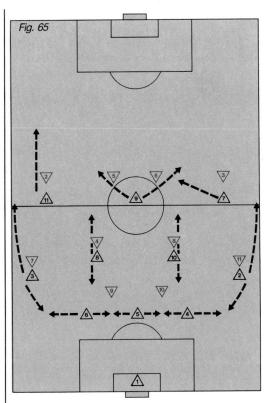

Fig. 65

Fig. 65 Three centre-backs
In this formation the three centre-backs ⟁, ⟁ and ⟁ are operating a zonal defence system, making it 3 v. 2 with the opposition's strikers. The full-backs push in and mark the wingers tightly, making it 4 v. 4 midfield. Up front there are three, and one of the wide men works inside diagonally to support the centre-forward.

Fig. 66 The sweeper system
Tight man-for-man marking all over the pitch is the key to this system, with the sweeper as the insurance.

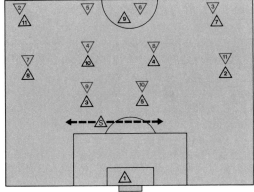

Fig. 66

When it is necessary to move up, someone, preferably the centre-half, should give the order. There should be plenty of talking to and from the goalkeeper.

Three centre-backs

A variation of the zonal system is the three centre-half idea used occasionally by Kenny Dalglish at Liverpool and Howard Wilkinson at Sheffield Wednesday. When opposed by teams with two big centre-forwards, Liverpool used Gary Gillespie, Mark Lawrenson and Alan Hansen as centre-backs, with the full-backs moving into midfield.

It enabled Liverpool to still have four players in midfield and three in attack. The centre-backs operated on a zonal basis and none of them was used as a sweeper. It is a modern interpretation of the zonal system.

The sweeper system

The other defensive system is the one used by most Continental sides, the Italian and West German style of a sweeper, or *libero*, playing behind three defenders who mark man-for-man and follow their opponent wherever he goes. The sweeper, or 'free' man, is responsible for covering the three markers. Any balls played through, or over their heads, he has to intercept. And if any player breaks through, it will be his job to challenge him.

He is the insurance, the spare man who gives the other defenders confidence to mark tight and get tackles in. The coach or manager will tell each defender whom to mark. The markers will aim to be much tighter than the average English defender, who has to be cautious because he knows there is no cover behind him. When they go abroad, players like Ian Rush, Mark Hateley and Gary Lineker find the sweeper system much harder to play against. They take time to get used to it.

In the zonal system, patience is called for, because if a defender fails in his challenge, his opponent pulls everyone out of position. So in English football, there is more jockeying, or holding off, than on the Continent.

In Europe, defenders will be constantly trying to win the ball in front of forwards as well as tackling from behind. When the ball is played up to the forward, they will try to get it ahead of the forward. In England, that does not happen as much because if he fails to reach the ball first, the defender knows he has put his team in trouble.

Tackling from behind has been virtually eliminated in England, except where defenders manage to reach the ball cleanly without touching an opponent. But in countries like West Germany and Spain, referees still tolerate it.

The weakness of the sweeper system is that defenders can be pulled out of position by forwards who are determined to do plenty of running off the ball. Midfield players have to be vigilant and ready to track back. Because the defence can be forced to lose its shape, the English and Brazilians prefer the more traditional zonal system.

The positive side to the sweeper system is that the sweeper is not merely a defender who stays back. Most of the better players in this position will join in attacks. Franz Beckenbauer was a pioneer in this field, often coming forward to create chances and score goals. Morten Olsen fulfils a similar function with the Danish side.

The Belgian system

A variation of the sweeper system is the one used by the Belgians most successfully in the

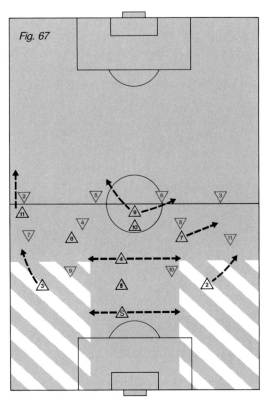

Fig. 67

Fig. 67 The Belgian system
The three defenders △, △ and △ are operating a zonal defence system, supported by the sweeper. △ is the anchor man midfield. There are only two forwards, △ and △, and one winger △. The striker △ is supported by the △.

1986 World Cup: a sweeper playing behind three zonal markers. It combined the advantages of both the Continental and the English methods and their defenders were not pulled out of position.

The Danish system

Another variation was the one employed by the USSR, France and Denmark, with a sweeper behind two markers and a five-man midfield. The Danes used Michael Laudrup, playing just behind the sole front player, Preben Elkjaer, and it was a most effective system. Opposing teams found it hard to counter because of the preponderance of players in midfield.

Tottenham used a similar system, except they operated with a normal zonal defence instead of a sweeper. Success with this system, as with any system, depends on the individual defender and whether he is good at his job. The system is only as good as those playing it.

The 'Funnel' System of Defence

No defensive system will ever stop goals being scored, but sound organisation can cut down the number of goals conceded.

One of the methods used by clubs like Arsenal and Liverpool is the 'funnel' system, where opponents are 'funnelled' into crowded areas in the centre of the pitch.

Wide defenders stand on the touchline side of their opponents, forcing them to go inside. In the years after the Second World War, full-backs were encouraged to do the opposite and show their opponents the line. But if they were beaten, it meant the winger could have a clear run down the flank, unless a centre-half came over to cover, and get a cross in. Even if the centre-half covered, it meant that the defence would be weakened in the middle.

Viv Anderson and Kenny Sansom invariably try to make their opponents move towards the centre of the pitch by taking up a position on the touch-line side.

The advantages of this system are that it stops opponents getting crosses in; it makes it unnecessary for central defenders to be pulled out of position and the edge of the penalty-box can be held, allowing attacking players to be caught offside.

If the ball is played behind the back-four, the goalkeeper can come out and get it. The flanks become prohibited areas and, as most goals come from crosses, it is logical that the number of goals conceded will decrease.

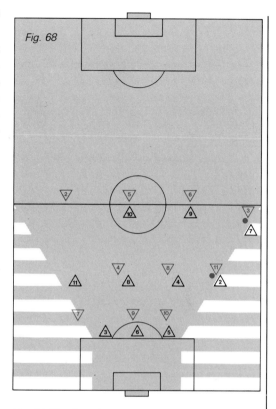

Fig. 68

Fig. 68 The funnel system
When ▽ or ▽ get the ball they are pushed into congested areas of the pitch by the defence, to prevent them making forward passes.

Defending as an Individual

Defending calls for intelligence and all the best defenders have been intelligent players. The contest between the defender and the opponent from whom he is trying to take the ball becomes a battle of wits. A wrong move by the defender, and the battle is lost.

Patience and concentration are needed. The good defender knows when to be tight on his opponent and when to drop off a little. His two main responsibilities are to mark and to cover, and the successful defender is the man who can perform both tasks equally well.

Arsenal and Liverpool have long had

reputations for being difficult sides to score against. This is because the players are brought up to use good defensive habits.

The principles of sound defensive play are:

1 The defender should aim to get close to the attacker as the ball arrives. He should not delay so that he arrives after the ball gets to his opponent. To close down, he must travel as the ball travels. If the attacker's control is poor and the ball bounces away from him, the defender is in a position to take the ball off him. But he will not be if he is too far away.

2 The defender should be balanced and in a position to make a tackle. His eyes should be focused on the ball, not on his opponent. He should be in the 'alert' position.

3 The defender should aim to prevent the attacker from passing the ball forward. He should be trying to restrict his opponent's passing angles. He will know at this point, or soon after, which is the weaker foot of his opponent and he will strive to make the attacker go on to that foot. The defender will be trying to make his adversary do what he wants by pushing him inside or outside.

4 The defender must be prepared to hold his ground, waiting for his opponent to move. He can pretend to tackle, just as the attacker makes diversionary movements. But he must be patient and not act prematurely or 'dive in'. When he makes his

Don't let him turn
When balls are played up to forwards, it is poor defending for a marking defender to allow his man to come away and turn.

Good markers, mainly central defenders, get close to the forward, roughly an arm's length away, in the 'alert' position. If the forward tries to turn, they either toe the ball away or put in a sliding block tackle, jabbing the leg out.

move, he must be sure that the odds favour him.

5 The aim of the defending side will be to keep play in front of them.

6 By closing down and holding up the opponent, the defender gives time to a colleague to cover behind him. And he also gives himself space to jockey back into.

7 He should strive to remain on his feet. The defender who commits himself and finds himself on the ground is out of the game temporarily and no use to his side.

8 Should the opponent 'give and go', the defender should ignore the ball and go with the runner so that the opponent cannot get a return pass.

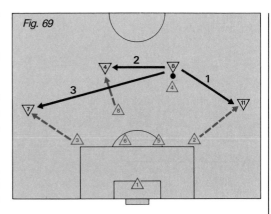

Fig. 69 Defending as an individual – travel as the ball travels
Pass 1 – △ closes ▽ down.
Pass 2 – △ closes ▽ down.
Pass 3 – △ closes ▽ down.

Adams closes down on Barnes, nice and low, eyes on the ball. When he gets the chance, he toes the ball away.

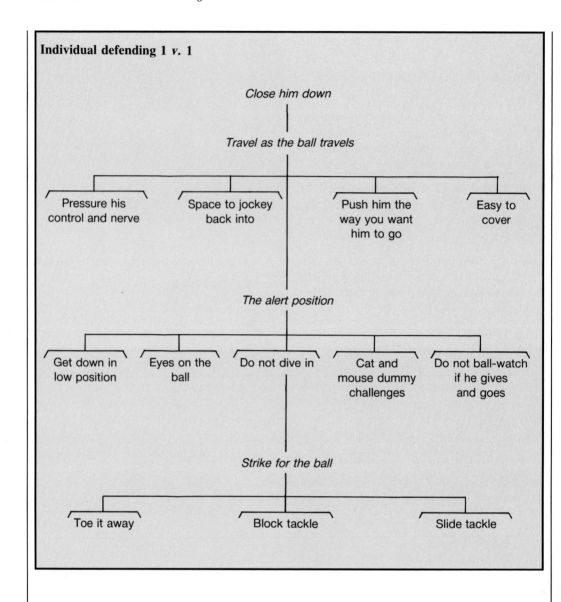

Individual defending 1 v. 1

Close him down

Travel as the ball travels

Pressure his control and nerve | Space to jockey back into | Push him the way you want him to go | Easy to cover

The alert position

Get down in low position | Eyes on the ball | Do not dive in | Cat and mouse dummy challenges | Do not ball-watch if he gives and goes

Strike for the ball

Toe it away | Block tackle | Slide tackle

Stance

It is important to consider the defender's stance when he is in a jockeying position. He should be in a semi-crouched position, ready to give chase if the attacker tries to push the ball past him.

Kenny Sansom, the Arsenal and England left-back, provides an object-lesson in how to approach the job the right way. Kenny gets low over the ball. If you are low, you are less inclined to fall for dummies and feints.

The head should be still and upright, not leaning to the left or right. Crouching for long periods is demanding on the legs and a defender needs to have powerful thighs. Weight training to develop the muscles is an important aid to be recommended.

(*Left*) *The jockeying position*
Adams is nice and low in the alert
position, pushing Barnes the way
he wants him to go.

Defending at the Front (Pressing or Hustling)

> **Winning the ball back in the opponents' half pays dividends.**

It has been proved that the more times you win the ball back in the opponents' half, the more goalscoring chances you will create. An outstanding exponent of this tactic, as he proved in Mexico, is Peter Beardsley.

The reasons why this tactic is successful are:

1 The nearer you win the ball back to the opposition's goal, the quicker you can strike at their goal.

2 There will be fewer opponents behind the ball, making the route to goal easier.

3 The more pressure you put on defenders, the more mistakes they will make.

Hustling is done both on an individual and collective basis and needs plenty of planning on the training ground. The correct mental attitude and fitness standards are of the utmost importance. Without these qualities, pressuring will fail.

The mental factor

The players, especially forwards, have to learn to switch their thinking – in possession, out of possession – instantly. When possession changes hands and the other team get the ball, there is a breakdown period.

That breakdown period will be shorter if the players can quickly adjust. Time is lost if players are caught up in other thoughts such as:

1 *Disappointment* – Perhaps a pass or a dribble has broken down. Some players want to show their disappointment. Their heads drop. They will try to explain to a colleague what went wrong. They might even fall over!

2 *Argument* – Sometimes misunderstandings occur. Players will stand and argue rather than apply pressure.

3 *Fitness* – Having worked hard attacking, a player does not have the condition to go again and pressure opponents.

4 *Idleness* – There are players who do not have the attitude to want to keep working when possession is lost.

5 *Superior attitude* – Some have the opinion that they are above chasing and pressuring opponents. They believe other players not as good as themselves should do that less glamorous job.

Fatigue affects thinking and skill. A tired player will make wrong decisions. Understanding will break down with team-mates.

Individual approach to pressuring

If his mental attitude is good, the player must get the approach right. The principles are:

1 The nearest man closes the opponent with the ball down. He chases back.

2 He will seek to prevent his opponent playing the ball forward by getting close and in front of him. He should get low and

spread his arms in a balanced position. And most important, he should not dive in.

3 He should force the opponent to play square or try and dribble his way out of trouble. In other words, he should make him take chances.

Every forward player should train and work at these methods to ensure the individual approach becomes a habit.

The collective approach to pressuring

There is a saying: 'Don't admire hustling, support it.' If the individual is doing his job, he needs the support of his team-mates to mark opponents in the pressure area and pick up and intercept square passes. Then having regained possession, they must counter-attack quickly.

The strategy should be:
1 Hustle
2 Regain possession
3 Counter-attack

Team tactics for pressuring

Football clubs at the professional level work hard at tactics on pressuring or guiding the opposition into less dangerous attacking areas. In general these tactics fall into two categories:

1 Letting a certain player have the ball.
2 Letting the opponents attack into certain parts of the pitch.

Letting a certain player have possession
This is a tactic Billy Bingham used with Northern Ireland and it played an important part in many of his team's successes. The Irish played with two wingers and a central striker, and before the game they would decide which of the opposing team's central defenders they would 'let out'. It would be

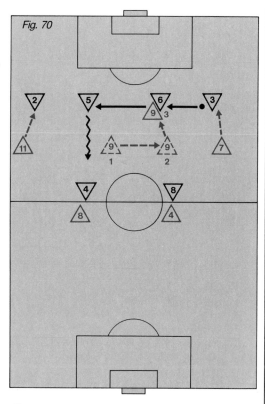

Fig. 70 Letting a certain player have possession
When the defending team have the ball, their opponents may let the player with the least ability ▽ take possession, hoping that he will make a mistake passing and give the ball away.

the one with the least ability on the ball, the man who might panic and lose possession.

Letting the opponents attack into certain areas of the pitch
First Division clubs have many ideas on team pressuring but the most common one is to let the opponents attack through and down the centre of the pitch and then squeeze back and put pressure man-on-man.

Because there are not enough good players at centre-back this tactic is successful, but when or if we develop centre-backs who are comfortable on the ball, this tactic will not be so effective.

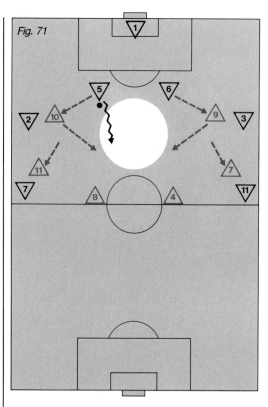

Fig. 71 Letting the opponents attack into certain areas of the pitch
The two front players, ▲ and ▲ pull wide, shutting off the full-backs and allowing the centre-backs to attack through the middle. When one of the centre-backs ▽ goes forward with the ball, the two strikers then squeeze back into the middle, putting pressure on ▽.

When are the best times to apply pressure?

It is virtually impossible to hustle for the whole ninety minutes but the following times can be vital:

1 *The first fifteen minutes*. This provides a good beginning and attitude to the game and ensures that your side takes the initiative. If the opponents make a slow start, your team can take advantage by getting an early goal. It also means your players are fresh and fit and ready to keep up the pressure.

2 *If your team has scored, the next fifteen*

minutes. When you have scored, the other team wants to reply straight away and very often it does. If you hustle well and get possession, there is little the opposition can do.

3 *The first ten minutes of the second half.* Once more it is important to get on top early and run the game. Some teams find it very difficult to get going again at the start of the second half. Cash in if this is the case.

> A good defence is like a Rolls-Royce engine. It is dependent on its smallest and least considered part.

The Point Man

In ice hockey there is a player who is known as the 'point man' and it is an idea that is being used more nowadays in football. Liverpool used it very effectively when Graeme Souness was on their staff.

Souness positioned himself about fifteen yards back in the central midfield position, and if play was congested down one side, he would call for the ball and direct it down the other side of the pitch where there was more space. It proved to be a better and safer way of switching the ball from one side of the pitch to the other.

Steve McMahon took over the Souness role and is equally good at it. The point man does not always switch the ball out wide. If there is space in front of him, he can advance and try a shot at goal or attempt a wall pass with one of his strikers.

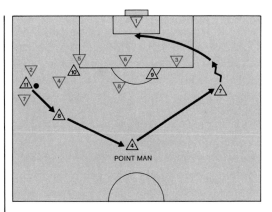

Fig. 72

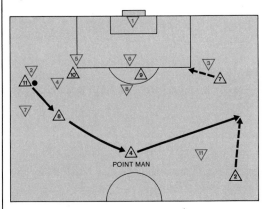

Fig. 72 Two examples of changing the play off the point man

Switching Play

Another tactic, not used enough in English football, also involves switching the play from one side of the pitch to the other. It is common on the Continent where teams invariably employ a sweeper.

Teams will attack down one side, pull the sweeper to cover that side of his defence, and then switch play in one or two passes to the other side to make a quick strike before the sweeper can adjust his position.

Offside

One of the reasons why English clubs do not use the sweeper is that they prefer to exploit the offside law to squeeze up and keep the team compact. England, Holland and Sweden are among the few countries doing this and when it was suggested to FIFA that the offside law should be amended to make it more difficult to trap opponents, a leading FIFA official replied, 'Why should it be altered just for two or three countries?'

The trend in the Football League is for the back-four to push up behind the play and take the action as far away as possible from their own goal. If the other side uses the same tactic, which is often the case, it means that the space in the centre of the pitch is limited to a twenty- or thirty-yard corridor. This can produce unskilful football, with the flow of passing constantly breaking down.

It means that forwards have to be alert for defenders moving up in an attempt to put them in an offside position. It also encourages forwards to try and take their opponents on. If they are successful, they usually have a free run at goal because there is no one behind the back-four covering. Good-thinking forwards will beat offside tactics, and many goals in England come from offside play breaking down.

Exploiting the offside law is like everything else – done to excess it can be harmful. The advantages are that it enables the team to remain compact, with the players in close support of each other. If a move breaks down, players are not in isolation as the opposition attack. More important, it can help a team win a game, by restricting the opposing side's attacking options.

On the other hand, there is the threat that if one player in the back-four fails to respond to the signal to move up, he can put an opponent onside and it could result in conceding a goal.

Liverpool, Arsenal and Everton use it to good effect and one successful advocate of offside tactics was Terry Venables before he went to Spain. He asked his defenders to push right up to the half-way line, a move which required great discipline and understanding.

Most teams will hold firm on the edge of the penalty-area and try to put opponents in an offside position. If the ball is played behind them, the goalkeeper is expected to act as a sweeper and clear it. Bruce Grobbelaar is good at this, just as Ray Clemence was before him at Liverpool.

The Sweeper

More countries use a sweeper system in defence than the square back-four traditionally favoured by English clubs. The sweeper, or last defender, has the responsibility for intercepting passes and runs which have eluded the marking defenders in front of him. He has to be clever at anticipating events or 'reading' the play. He also has to be a good tackler.

Some English clubs, like Southampton, have used the sweeper system for a number of years, and since Kenny Dalglish took over at Liverpool he has used it when the occasion demanded. This is usually when Liverpool are confronted by a team which has quick forwards, like West Ham.

In the past, the sweeper has been a predominantly defensive player but the success of Franz Beckenbauer, formerly a midfield player, in the position showed that the sweeper could be the team's most effective attacking player. Beckenbauer had the ability to go forward and fill the role of an extra attacker. Other countries followed his lead. Ruud Krol performed a similar role with the outstanding Holland side of the Seventies; Alexander Chivadze did it in the USSR side and Maxime Bossis was used in the same way in the French side of the Eighties.

No longer was the sweeper looked upon as a purely negative player. One of the advantages of using him in an attacking role was that he was rarely picked up by opposing players. He was the spare man, a player who was comfortable on the ball and could use it profitably.

Despite the obvious advantages of the system, it has still not caught on in Britain to any great extent.

Some sides use a defensive player in front of their back-line as an anchor man, or 'screen' player. Liverpool did this for years with Graeme Souness, who was not only a redoubtable tackler but an excellent user of the ball. Italy did it with Tardelli, Holland with Neeskens and, in recent years, France with Luis Fernandez. Steve McMahon has taken over the role at Anfield with considerable success.

The main job of the anchor man is to pick the danger off before it becomes a threat to the markers behind him. The player performing this role has to be a ball-winner and also a good user of the ball. One of his main tasks is to prevent the ball being played to the feet of the forwards.

Pressing

In basketball there is a tactic called the *full* press and it is now used in soccer. The idea is to press up to the half-way line and deny the opposition space in their own half. The team is kept in a compact shape and pressure is kept on the other team. The *full* press also takes the play as far as possible from the team's own goal.

The Continentals favour the *half* press. When they lose possession of the ball, their players will drop back into their own half to put as many defenders as possible between the ball and their goal. They will seek to regain possession in their own half and start advancing again, exploiting the spaces created by drawing the opposition forward.

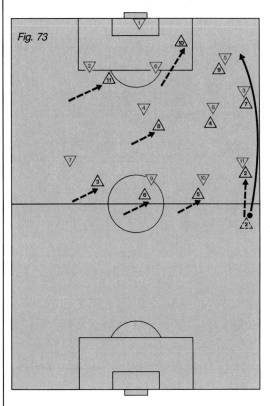

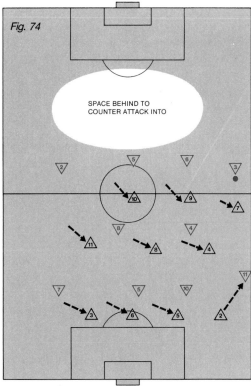

Fig. 73 The full press
An example of this tactic, squeezing all space and outlets in the opponents' half.

Fig. 74 The half press
The main advantages of the half press are: a) It makes it difficult for the opponents to attack through crowded areas. b) It is easier for the defending team to cover and support each other in tackling situations.

Tackling

Tackling is and always has been an important part of the game. Nowadays players all over the pitch are expected to be able to win the ball, not just defenders. When the ball is lost, everyone becomes a defender.

British players still tend to be superior in this department to Continental and South American players, although there are some outstanding tacklers in other parts of the world. The public likes to see a properly executed tackle, and there has been no better sight in the game than Nobby Stiles, the former Manchester United and England player, winning the ball. Bobby Moore, the ex-captain of West Ham and England, was another excellent tackler but he relied on timing as much as strength. Of today's players, Mark Lawrenson is probably the

leading tackling defender in the game.

There are three main types of tackles:

1 The block tackle which is made in fifty-fifty situations in midfield areas when passes are underweighted or inaccurate.

2 The sliding tackle which is most frequently used by recovering defenders and sometimes by forwards tackling back.

3 The toe-away tackle used by defenders on forwards who are in screening positions with their backs to the defender. A good defender will always be looking for an opportunity to toe the ball away.

The Block Tackle

The essentials for a block tackle are:

1 It should be timed to meet the ball when the opponent is playing it.

2 The non-tackling foot should be placed to one side of and slightly behind the ball.

(Below) *The block tackle*
Getting his timing spot on, Adams goes in hard with the inside of the right foot, his body power in behind.

105

3 The force of the tackling foot is through the centre of the ball.

4 The tackle is made with the inside of the foot, which provides the largest blocking surface.

5 Both knees are slightly bent to absorb the shock of the impact. Small, stocky players of the build of Kenny Sansom have a distinct advantage in a block tackle because by having a lower position they can get more power into their tackle. Also their balance tends to be better than that of a bigger man.

6 The player making the tackle must go into it in a determined manner, using his full weight. A half-hearted challenge can sometimes result in injury or losing the ball.

7 The ankle should be firm, with the muscles tensed to take the extra strain.

8 The same principles apply to the block tackle from the side, but the tackler will want to get as close as possible to the ball before he commits himself. The non-tackling foot should be level or slightly ahead of the ball. Should the ball be lodged between the feet of the two players, it may be possible to lift it over the opponent's foot by pulling it up and over.

The Sliding Tackle

The sliding tackle is a more desperate measure than the block tackle because it will leave the tackling player on the ground. It is imperative that he succeeds in winning the ball or putting it away to safety. If he does not, he has imperilled his goal and has no chance of recovery.

Sliding tackles are usually made by full-backs or back-four defenders who are chasing after players who have broken clear.

(Below) *The sliding tackle*
Adams gets his foot ahead and wraps it round the ball.

The essentials of the sliding tackle are:

1 The eyes must be on the ball.

2 The tackler must be as near as possible to his target.

3 His tackling leg will, on most occasions, be the one further away from his opponent and he will try to 'wrap' it around the ball to win it, or knock it away with the studs or instep. But the tackle can also be performed with the nearest leg contacting the ball with the outside of the boot.

4 The tackling leg should start off in a position slightly ahead of the ball. If this does not happen, the tackler will connect

with the opponent's foot and give away a foul.

5 The tackling leg should be low and close to the ground but not totally straight. Closeness to the ground ensures there is no injury.

6 The other leg will be doubled up for balance and to avoid contact with the opponent's legs.

7 The arm on the tackling side will be stretched out to meet the ground and soften the fall.

8 The strike for the ball is vital.

(*Below*) Manchester United's Jesper Olsen is tackled by Ajax Amsterdam defender Ronald Spelbos.

Practices for tackling

Fig. 75 Closing down and jockeying
Player △ passes to △ then follows the ball and practises jockeying. △ passes to △, follows the ball and practises jockeying. △ passes to △ and so on.

Fig. 76 The block tackle
A grid area is marked out with cones. Player △ dribbles with the ball. He is tackled by △ and attempts to pass the ball to △. The players then change places.

The sliding tackle
Fig. 77 The coach ▽ kicks the ball in a straight line on the right-hand side of the touch-line. The three players on the right take it in turns to run after the ball and slide it across the touch-line before it reaches the goal-line. The practice is repeated on the other side.
Fig. 78 This is similar to the first practice, except this time there is a player, instead of the coach, dribbling with the ball, and other players take it in turns to slide-tackle him.

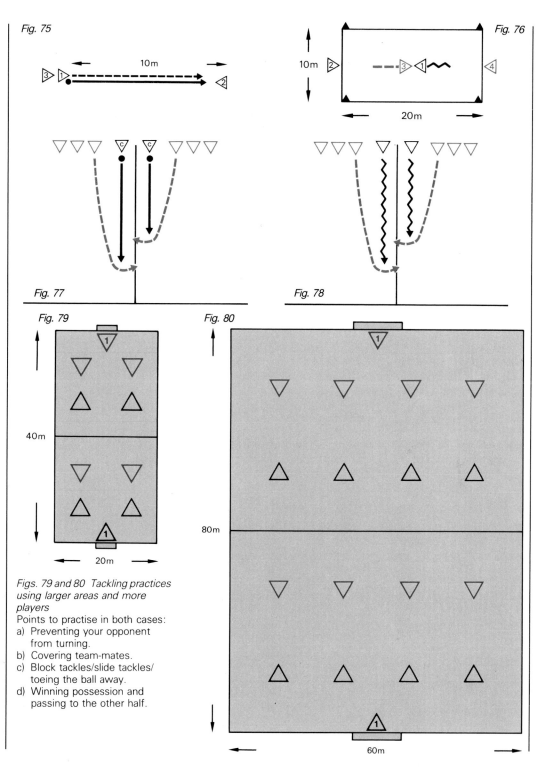

Fig. 75

Fig. 76

Fig. 77

Fig. 78

Fig. 79

Fig. 80

Figs. 79 and 80 Tackling practices using larger areas and more players

Points to practise in both cases:
a) Preventing your opponent from turning.
b) Covering team-mates.
c) Block tackles/slide tackles/ toeing the ball away.
d) Winning possession and passing to the other half.

Toeing the Ball Away

This is another way of dispossessing a forward who has his back to the defender. The defender should crouch down in the 'alert' position. He should not let the forward turn. He should not get too close. But he should be alert for opportunities to shoot out a leg and toe the ball away from the opponent without giving away a foul.

Attitudes

Success in tackling depends to a large degree on the attitude of the player. The strong, determined player will gain possession more than the one who is timid. Tackling techniques can be taught as in any other skill but they have to be accompanied by a will to win the ball.

The tackler has to follow through with the full weight of his body. The more of his weight behind the tackle, the greater the chance the ball will break for him. As coaches say, 'Put your foot in!'

Heading

Heading has always been an important part of the game, more so in Britain than in the rest of the world. The Football League has produced more players who are good at heading than almost any other League because the ball is in the air more in the British game.

This is one of the reasons why Italian clubs have bought players from England over the years, from John Charles to Mark Hateley. They have all been outstanding in the air. This tradition of goalscorers who score many of their goals with the head has been carried on from Dixie Dean, Tommy Lawton and Nat Lofthouse to today's strikers, notably Graeme Sharp, John Fashanu, Garry Thompson, Mark Falco and Mark Hateley.

I must say, however, that there are fewer players around these days who lead in this field. Like most skills, the art of heading is mastered through developing a good technique and practising it.

If you throw a ball to a young boy and ask him to head it, he will close his eyes and not be too happy about it because heading is not an act that comes naturally. But with patience he will soon overcome his fears and learn to enjoy it.

When practising heading, I always recommend that the pressure of the ball is reduced slightly. No one likes heading a hard ball. In the old days it was possible to cut the head by hitting the lace but today's balls are much better, with no laces, just a small pin-hole.

How to Head the Ball

Contact should be made on the hairline in the centre of the forehead. That is the toughest part of the scalp. Some players use the side of the head. Alan Gilzean late of Tottenham, was probably the greatest exponent of that art but he only mastered it after years of practice. He made a difficult heading skill look easy.

If you want to head to the side, the best course is to turn the head in the direction in which you want the ball to go and direct it. That way you are watching the ball all the time. It is sometimes said that the eyes should remain open, even on contact. But it is natural to close the eyes for a split second when the head hits the ball.

Heading by Defenders

Many times in a game it will be necessary for players in the back-four to head clear, long kicks and dangerous crosses from the opposing goalkeeper or defender. The object must be to head the ball powerfully out of danger and to do that requires certain techniques from the player.

1 He has to judge the flight of the ball.

2 He has to time his jump to reach the ball at the highest possible point.

3 He will need to make a run of one or two steps before taking off on one leg.

4 The body must be balanced at take-off, with the torso leaning backwards, the arms outstretched in front and the head inclined backwards.

5 On impact the body will be punching forwards towards the ball and through the arms.

6 This thrusting, forward motion will provide power and distance in the header.

Heading by defenders

(*Above*) Jumping early, Adams gets above Barnes. With his eyes on the ball, he powers it away.

(*Right*) Everton's Kevin Ratcliffe shows the value of a good jump as he rises above six-feet four-inch George Reilly when Reilly was with Watford.

The technique can be practised without an opponent initially but a slightly different approach will be needed when going up with a forward. It will become necessary to turn the body slightly, leading towards the flight of the ball with whichever shoulder the player finds more convenient.

This will help to protect him from facial injury on body contact. But even with the shoulder leading, centre-halves and back-four players sometimes find they get knocks as their head comes into contact with the back of the forward's head.

The player's aim must be to get as high as possible, above the opponent who is likely to be backing into him. Some defenders will spread their arms to show the referee that they are not fouling.

The centre-back who dominates his penalty-box in the air is vital in the English League and over the years the successful teams have all possessed one – Ron Yeats, Maurice Norman, Brian Labone and Jack Charlton, to name but a few.

Heading away crosses

As most goals come from crosses, the defender's strategy must be to clear every cross that comes into the box. When the ball is in the air, the defender must ensure that

he is in the 'angle' position, half-facing the direction of the ball but also keeping his immediate opponent in view by turning his shoulder.

To watch only the ball and ignore the opponent is often fatal. If it is a normal, far-post cross, his aim must be to head the ball away as far as possible outside the box. He will want to be first to the ball.

But if the cross is a hanging one to the back of him, he will have to adjust his position. Two courses of action are open to him:

1 He can turn and flick the ball away across to the far side of the pitch, using the pace of the cross to help it on.

2 He can head it back to the goalkeeper or a colleague.

Both are split-second decisions with risks attached. Wherever possible, he must aim to get the ball away and out of danger, and if possible, set up a counter-attack. A constructive header is better than just heading anywhere.

Heading away crosses
For balance in the air, Adams spreads his legs, powering the ball away.

Attacking Heading

Forward players are required to head the ball as often as defenders but the techniques they use are different. Whereas the defender aims for height and distance to clear the ball, the forward directs the ball either to a colleague or in a strike on goal.

Most forwards will be striving to get in front of defenders to get their header in first. When it comes to scoring goals, they will not wait for the ball to come to them, they will go to meet it.

Heading the long kick

The forward will either flick the ball on to a runner or direct it back to a midfield player. These are two techniques which are available to the front player.

Another technique is used by tall players like Niall Quinn, who will push back against the centre-half, denying him a running jump at the ball. He will time his jump to contact the ball on the top of his head, flicking it behind him over the centre-half to a forward-running colleague.

A forward heading the ball back is not seen so often in the modern game but it is a useful skill, particularly around the penalty-area. The late Tommy Taylor was an expert at it.

Heading for goal

The bulk of attacking headers at goal come from positions on the near post – known as the goalkeeper's nightmare because he can never reach the ball first – and the far or back post and beyond. There are also attacking headers from the centre of goal by players who have got free of their markers. Far-post headers are for players coming in behind defenders, like Mark Hateley and Frank Stapleton who can outjump opponents and head with power and accuracy. Near post headers are the speciality of players like Gary Lineker and Clive Allen, who time their runs correctly.

Far-post header

The attacking player will be directing his header *downwards* at two vulnerable points, either back across goal inside the opposite post or down towards the inside of the near post (*Fig. 80*).

1 He will be facing the direction in which he intends to put the ball.

2 He will time his run to make sure he arrives at the same time as the ball, getting there ahead of his marker whom he will be attempting to shake off by checking in the opposite direction first.

(*Left*) Heading is a dangerous business and here Arthur Albiston and Andy Gray show how determination is needed in aerial challenges.

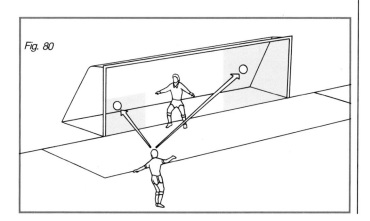

Fig. 80

3 He will be aiming to get up and over the line of flight, so that he can propel the ball with power at the target.

Near-post header (*Fig. 81*)

The near-post header is a more delicate skill. It gained widespread use after Ron Greenwood picked it up from the Hungarians and used it successfully at West Ham. The forward needs a good understanding with the player making the cross and Greenwood had this with Geoff Hurst and Martin Peters.

The ball is dealt a glancing blow and the forward uses the pace of the cross to help it on its way. The forward needs to make space for himself by checking back and timing his run right.

1 Ball and man must arrive together.

2 As the goalkeeper will be on his near post, the chances of scoring are greater if the header can be directed back across the unprotected part of the goal.

The diving header

Often the ball will not arrive at a convenient height and the forward has to dive to reach it. Agility, determination and courage are needed and two players who personify these are Bryan Robson and Gary Mabbutt.

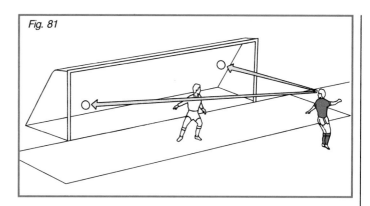

(*Left*) A classic illustration of the power-header at goal by England captain Bryan Robson. He is seen scoring England's second goal against France in their 3–1 win in Bilbao. The other players are Christian Lopes and goalkeeper Jean Luc Ettori. The temperature in the San Mames Stadium was 110°F.

Fig. 81

Heading Practices for Young Players

Aims of coach:

> Good technique.
> Conquer the fear of heading.
> Balance in the air.

a) Throw up, head to partner.

b) Throw to partner – he heads back. (Vice versa after ten goes.)

c) As previous practice, but the throws must be to the left and right of the header.

d) One player in small goal throws to partner – he heads to try and score.

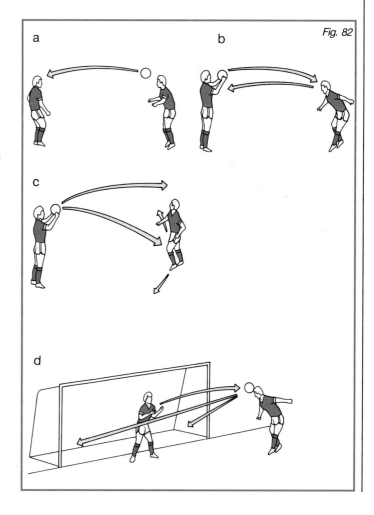

Fig. 82

e) Keep the ball in the air by heading to each other.

f) In threes – 1 throws, 3 stands in front of 2, 2 must jump over and above 3 to head back to 1.

g) In threes – 1 throws to 2, he heads and directs the ball to 3. (3 must be on the move.)

h) In goals – 1 crosses to 2, 2 heads and tries to score past 3.

i) Heading crosses away – 1 crosses to 2, he must head the ball out of the box to 3.

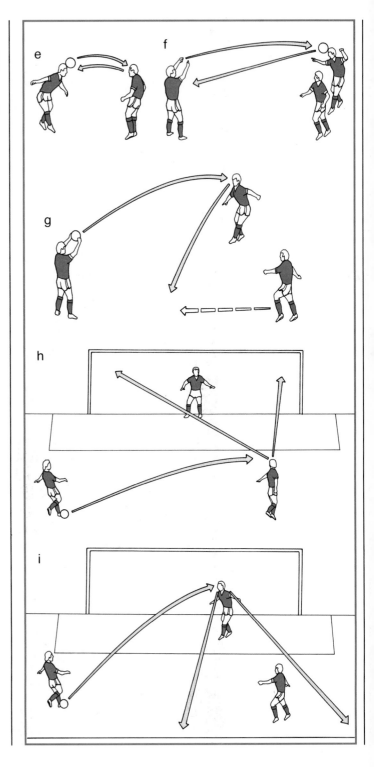

(*Opposite*) England's Neil Webb dives to head towards goal.

Set Plays

Goal-Kicks

Goal-kicks from the six-yard box

Most goalkeepers should practise to be able
to reach the half-way line with their kicks.
The technique used by the goalkeeper to
kick the ball from the ground will be the
same as described in the section on passing
the ball, in particular that of the lob pass
with the toe scraping the ground (see p. 38).

The goalkeeper will be going for distance,
aiming at one of his forwards or a player
whom he thinks is weakest in the air in the
opposing back-four.

His three main options are:

1 To aim in his attack for the big man who is
best in the air. Other players in his team will
surround the big man in what is known as
the 'knock-down' area. The centre-forward
will try to flick the ball on to a colleague or
knock it down to a midfield player.

2 The short goal-kick. As the other players
move out, a full-back will drop back to
receive a short goal-kick and play the ball
back to the goalkeeper. The goalkeeper can
then obtain extra distance from a kick out of
the hands. The opposing side will be on the
look-out for the short kick, so there are
dangers. Alert forwards can cut the ball out
and create a goal-scoring chance for themselves.

3 Aim wide to one of the opponents' full-
backs. The advantages of kicking wide to
the flank is that the full-back's range is
restricted. He is forced to head the ball
infield or out for a throw. It is hard for
opponents to attack from this position.

Goal-kicks out of the hands

There are two methods of drop-kicking; the
low trajectory half-volley which is used to
good effect by Ray Clemence and David
Seaman among others, and the full volley
which is known among goalkeepers as 'the

Fig. 83 Goal-kick tactics – winning zonal knock-downs
⚠,⚠,⚠ and ⚠ know exactly where the ball is going
to be kicked. They push in and surround that area. The
big centre-forward ▽ challenges for the ball as it
descends. If he flicks it on, the ▽ goes for it. Should
the defender ⚠ head it, he will not get much power in
the header because he is under pressure. That is when
the ⚠, ⚠, ⚠ and ⚠ can get the knock-down and start
an attack.

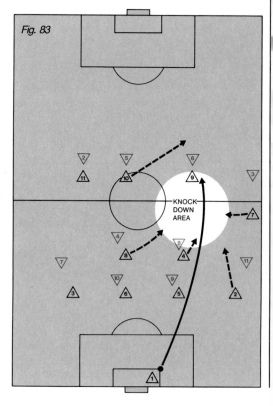

Fig. 83

(*Left*) Ray Clemence, then with Liverpool, shows the ideal technique for kicking the ball from the hands. The ball must not be thrown too high into the air.

Fig. 84 Goal-kicks out of the hands
If you have a goalkeeper with a good, high kick out of the hands, it is worth practising pushing up to take advantage of it:
a) Squeeze your opponents back into their half.
b) Push your team virtually into their half to win knock-downs and attack from there.
c) Go for flicks-on if the opposing back-four are square.

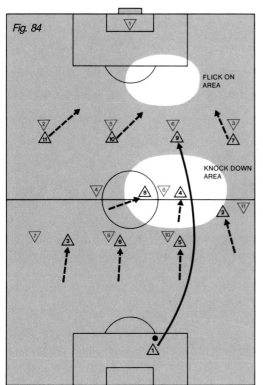

Fig. 84

FLICK ON AREA

KNOCK DOWN AREA

snow ball' because it goes so high that when it comes down it has snow on it!

Forwards will be looking to chest down the first type of kick or head it back to a colleague.

The high, dropping kick presents problems to defenders. They cannot head the ball back upfield because of the angle from which it drops at them and are likely to mishead it to the side. They may well not be able to head it properly, giving possession to the other side.

Two-footed kicking

It is essential that the goalkeeper is able to kick with both feet, because, if he is one-footed, the other team will sometimes detail a player to block him on his kicking side.

Pushing up on goal-kicks from the hands

With goalkeepers nowadays able to kick further distances because of the extra training

123

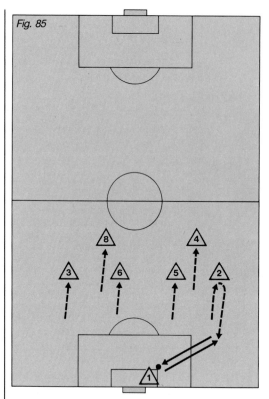

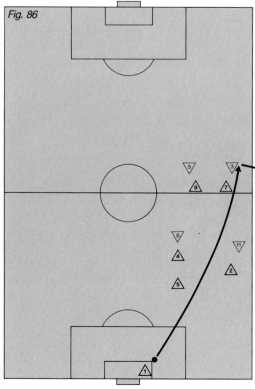

Fig. 85 The short goal-kick
The back-four push out as normal for a goal-kick. As the goalkeeper is placing the ball on the corner of the six-yard box he looks up. The full-back △ quickly doubles back, gets the ball outside the box and knocks it back to the goalkeeper, who then kicks it out of his hands. The full-back quickly gets up with the other back-four players.

Fig. 86 The goal-kick close to the touch-line
The goal-kick is aimed at the opponents' full-back ▽ whose position close to the touch-line limits him to a small range of heading possibilities. More times than not he opts to head out for a throw-in.

they undergo compared with goalkeepers of previous generations, it is possible for teams to push up into their opponents' half and take play as far as possible from their own goal.

Throw-Ins

There are more throw-ins during a game than any other form of restart, yet throw-ins are a neglected part of the teaching of the game. Goals often result from them, particu-larly long throws to the near post which are flicked on.

There are a number of basic principles about throws. Firstly, the throw should be taken quickly by the nearest player, unless there is a chance of a long throw into the box, in which case the team's specialist long thrower must be called into action.

The throw should be directed at any player who is unmarked. Players must create opportunities for themselves to receive the ball by intelligent movement, like cross-over runs which can block out markers.

The ball should be thrown forwards at all times unless there is a safe alternative. When a team gets a throw inside its own half, the taker will be looking to throw it down the line to take the danger away from his goal. If in a subsequent challenge the ball is put out of play, he has gained a number of yards.

Fig. 87 Cross-overs and blocking on throw-ins
A On the right side △ throws the ball. △ makes a wide run just missing △. △ plus the man marking him block ▽ and let △ get free down the line.
B On the left side the same principle applies with the △ getting free on the inside.

Fig. 88 Defending at throw-ins
The attacking team have a throw in. △ drops back and gets in front of ▽. △ drops back to mark ▽ and the centre-back △ acts as sweeper. △ is on hand should the ball be returned to ▽.

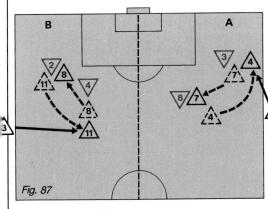

Fig. 87

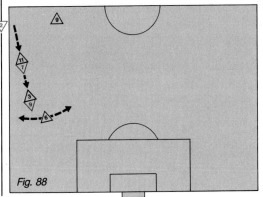

Fig. 88

The ball should be thrown in such a way that it is easy for the receiver to control it. Preferably, it should go to feet but if that is not possible, to the head or even the chest. The thrower should be looking to get the ball back.

It should be remembered that a throw is a pass, so it should have the same ingredients of a pass – accuracy, the right positioning and the right speed or weight.

The long throw

Most teams now have a long thrower. Ian Hutchinson of Chelsea and Bobby Woodruff of Swindon and Crystal Palace were pioneers of the idea in England. Kenny Sansom, Gary Stevens of Everton and Graham Roberts of Glasgow Rangers and late of Tottenham are among those in the modern generation who can reach the penalty-spot with throws.

The throw to the near post is hard to defend against. The attacking team will have one or two of its tallest men waiting for it, and their aim will be to flick the ball behind them for a colleague to put into the net.

England went ahead with this type of goal after twenty-seven seconds against France in the 1982 World Cup, when Terry Butcher knocked on a Sansom throw and Bryan Robson volleyed the ball in.

To obtain maximum distance, it is important to spread the hands around the ball with the thumbs almost touching. Some players stand with their feet together, using the body as a spring. Others stand with legs one in front of the other. Balance is important. With practice, every player should be able to attain a reasonable distance from long throws.

The harder the throw and the lower the trajectory, the more difficult it is for defenders to cope.

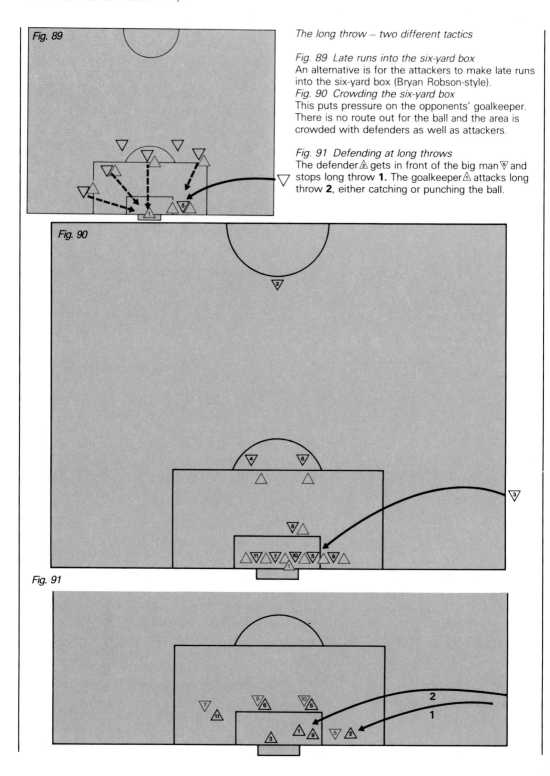

Fig. 89

The long throw – two different tactics

Fig. 89 Late runs into the six-yard box
An alternative is for the attackers to make late runs into the six-yard box (Bryan Robson-style).
Fig. 90 Crowding the six-yard box
This puts pressure on the opponents' goalkeeper. There is no route out for the ball and the area is crowded with defenders as well as attackers.

Fig. 91 Defending at long throws
The defender △ gets in front of the big man ▽ and stops long throw **1**. The goalkeeper △ attacks long throw **2**, either catching or punching the ball.

Fig. 90

Fig. 91

Free-Kicks

There are many ways of taking a free-kick, and so much thought now goes into it that it is almost an art. Most professional sides will spend a large part of a morning, usually Thursday, rehearsing their free-kicks.

The aim, naturally, is to score a goal from every free-kick, but this is not possible. One in ten is a more common ratio. If the free-kick is near enough to goal to enable the attacking side to mount a direct shot, then a shot should be attempted.

Some free-kick routines can be complicated but in general the simpler the idea, the more likely it is to succeed. One or two touches are better than three because when a wall is breaking to close down the person on the ball, time is space.

The longer it takes to execute the free-kick, the easier it is for the defending side to block it. Therefore, the direct shot, providing it is on target, often gives the best results. Most goals at free-kicks come from a bending shot or from an idea introduced into English football by Terry Venables called 'moving the free-kick' (*Fig. 92*).

Like most good ideas, the Venables one is a simple one. Two attackers stand over the ball while it is lined up. The kicker will tap it a short distance to his colleague who will stop it, enabling another team-mate from the rear to have a shot at the goal, which is now less protected because the shot is coming from a more favourable angle.

At every free-kick, the attacking side needs a 'general' – a man who organises the kick. He will give the instructions and be responsible for the timing. Two players should take part in the planning of the free-kick, one right-footed and the other left-footed. It will be beneficial if they can chip

Fig. 92

the ball accurately or, if the occasion demands it, use a powerful direct shot. Having practised two or three free-kicks in training, the general will decide which one to use in the match.

It used to be customary for bending free-kicks to be served round the end of the wall, or over the last man in the wall, but my thinking on this changed when I went to Paris several years ago to watch Michel Platini, one of the finest takers of free-kicks in the history of the game, in action against Peru. When France were awarded a free-kick on the right side of the box, I expected Platini to take it with his right foot. Instead, Bernard Genghini took it with his left foot, sending the ball over the inside of the wall and bending it back towards the near post and away from the goalkeeper.

When France had a free-kick on the left side of the box, Platini took it with his right foot, bending the ball inside the near post, again away from the goalkeeper. This method was so effective that England have since adopted it, and we use Glenn Hoddle for the right-footed free-kicks and a left-footed player, usually John Barnes if he is in the side, for the left-footed ones.

The pace and height of the kick have to be

right. If the ball is struck too slowly, the goalkeeper will have time to get across his goal to make a save. If it is struck too hard, it will fly over the crossbar. The French and Brazilians practise with wooden or metal frames representing players in a wall and some English clubs do this as well.

To deceive the opposition it is useful to have a player running over the ball to try and pull the goalkeeper out of position. If the goalkeeper is badly positioned, standing behind the wall instead of to the side of it where he would have a clear sight of the ball, it is possible to blast the ball into the gap. This requires pace and accuracy and another player may be called up to supply it. It is rare that one player is capable of taking a variety of free-kicks himself.

West Ham, for instance, have Tony Gale to take the benders and either Ray Stewart or Mark Ward to take the ones that require a hard-driven shot. Follow-up players are essential. If the ball rebounds off the goalkeeper or woodwork, they must be in position to tap it in.

Free-kicks from wide positions

Free-kicks taken from a wide position outside the box can be turned into effective weapons if the right service is provided. The most damaging type of free-kick is the one that bends towards the near post, either inswinging or outswinging.

Defenders find it difficult to counter because they are facing their own goal. The attacking player only needs a touch and a goal can result.

Should it be an inswinger or an outswinger?
More times than not, these decisions are made in training. But players on the ball must look for reasons to do one or the other in the game.

If you have two players on the ball, one

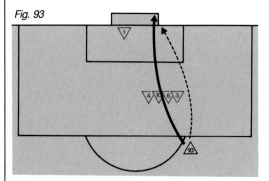

Fig. 93

Fig. 93 Free-kicks on the edge of the penalty box
The dotted line indicates the direction of the traditional type of free-kick, taken with the right foot, bending around the wall towards the goalkeeper. The unbroken line indicates the modern left-footed technique over the wall and bending away from the goalkeeper.

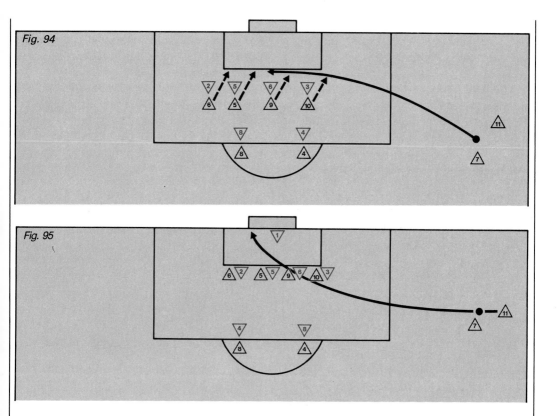

Fig. 94

Fig. 95

Fig. 94 Outswinging free-kick
The right-footed player △ takes the kick, bending the ball along the edge of the six-yard box for the attackers △ , △ , △ and △ to run onto.

Fig. 95 Inswinging free-kick
△ takes the kick, bending the ball in towards the centre of goal. The attackers △ , △ , △ and △ on the edge of the six-yard box get in front of defenders for a glancing header to score.

left-footed and the other right-footed, they can decide which course they should follow after assessing the position of the defenders.

If the defenders are well out from goal, they can outswing the ball behind the defenders.

If the defenders are deep, they can inswing the ball into crowded areas.

Indirect free-kicks

Outside the penalty-area, the same principles apply as at a direct free-kick when the ball is played to another player. Speed is essential, particularly in defence.

When an indirect free-kick is awarded within ten yards of the goal, all eleven players must line up on the goal-line. When the kick is taken, they will charge the ball, reducing the angle for the marksman.

The attacking side will want to play the ball back or, if the kick is in a wide position, closer to goal to improve the angle.

Defending at free-kicks (building the wall)

The onus is on the goalkeeper and an outfield player who is deputed to the task of positioning the wall. The outfield player should be the second man in the wall who, under the direction of the goalkeeper, should station himself in line with the near post. He should be facing the goalkeeper, turning to face the ball when the wall is in the correct position.

The first man, preferably a tall man, stands one man's width outside the wall to block the bending shot aimed around the post. The anchor man in second place should also be tall to counter the chip shot inside the post. The taller they are, the less chance the kicker has of chipping the ball effectively on target. The ball has to go higher and this allows the goalkeeper more time to get across to it.

The anchor man must make certain no one is pulling the wall out of place.

Defenders in a wall need to be brave and resolute. When the kick is taken they must not turn or duck; they must stand tall and take whatever is coming. One concession to

safety is that it is advisable to protect the private parts!

Some coaches recommend that the players in the wall should link arms. I do not subscribe to that view. It restricts movement. Once the kick is taken, it is the duty of the men in the wall to break out and help in the clearing-up work.

The best players to have in a wall are invariably midfield players and should be

nominated in advance. Defenders will be needed to mark opposing forwards and attackers will be back, picking up opposing central defenders. It is vital to have all eleven players back at free-kicks. If not, the defending side could find itself outnumbered with fatal consequences.

The goalkeeper has to trust his wall. If he does not and moves to the side of goal that the wall is protecting, he can be beaten in his space. This happened to Peter Shilton in an International in Paris once.

Another important figure in the defence is the 'charge-down' man who stands to the right of the wall just out of line with the far post. It is his job to run at the ball and attempt to block the free-kick. At Arsenal, Peter Storey had this role. With England it has usually been Ray Wilkins. It needs a fearless character.

Delay is important. Unless the defending side can hold up play, the free-kick can be quickly taken and the ball can end up in the net. The referee does not wait for the wall to be positioned to signal the taking of a kick.

Standing on the ball to prevent a restart is illegal, so what usually happens is that defenders will ignore the ball and position themselves while the opposition are retrieving it. The anchor man organising the wall must get himself in position immediately, and the wall is then built around him.

Once the free-kick is blocked, everyone must push out of the box as soon as possible.

(Left) Here is a good example of a soundly constructed wall on the edge of the box, as demonstrated by the England team in an international against France. The tallest man, Terry Butcher, is furthest to the line of the shot from Michel Platini, and in the six-man line-up next to him are Bryan Robson, Glenn Hoddle, Steve Williams, Brian Stein and Mike Duxbury. The idea of having the tallest man in that position is that his presence forces the kicker to aim his shot higher and that gives the goalkeeper more time to get across his goal and make a save. Sammy Lee (4) acts as the 'charge-down' man. He is responsible for 'charging' the ball as the kick is taken.

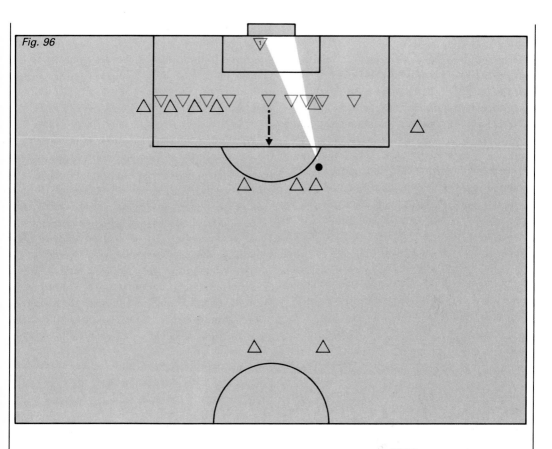

Fig. 96

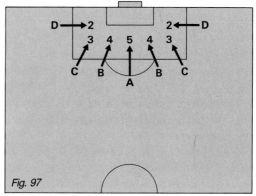

Fig. 97

(*Opposite, above*) An example of how a wall should *not* react at a free-kick. The five Spanish defenders playing against England in the 1982 World Cup show a distinct lack of bravery as Trevor Francis shoots. But the England forward was off-target and Spain survived to draw 0–0. Note the position of the goalkeeper. He is well placed to see the ball if it had come his side of the wall.

(*Opposite, below*) Gary Owen, second from left, showing how to organise a wall. He is the man on the line of the near post, facing the goalkeeper who tells him whether to put his colleagues to the left or right.

Fig. 96 Building the wall on free-kicks
The wall must guard one half of the goal and be positioned exactly. The second man in faces the goal and lines himself up with the near post. He has one man on his outside to prevent the curled shot around the wall. He has two tall men on his inside to block the shot and prevent the curled chip over the wall. There is also one player positioned just off the inside of the wall to close the shot down if necessary and another player positioned wide to protect the wing. Other defenders protect the far post in case of a far-post chip.

Fig. 97 How many men in the wall?
Peter Shilton works on these principles according to which position the kick is taken from:
A Centre of goal – five in the wall.
B Sides of the 'D' – four in the wall.
C Wide of the 'D' – three in the wall.
D Wide wing areas – two in the wall.

Taking Corner-Kicks

The player taking a corner-kick must be an accurate kicker of the ball. If he is not, it is a waste of time positioning men in the six-yard box and getting them to move around.

The player taking the kick must be capable of dropping the ball in a fairly precise area, and he has to overlook problems like a short, uphill run-up off a running track, or a scarred surface within the quadrant.

It is rare that one player can take all the corners on either side of the pitch. Glenn Hoddle has done it at Spurs but what usually happens is that a right-footed player, like England's Ray Wilkins, will take the corners from the left which will be natural inswingers, and a left-footed player, like John Barnes, will take them from the right.

Alan Hinton, the former Derby County winger, was one of the best corner-kickers in my time. He could almost drop the ball where he wanted it. Johnny Giles was another when he was with Leeds. Jack Charlton scored many goals from corners taken by Giles. This was the start of the tactic of the big centre-half standing close to the goal-line and beating the goalkeeper with a near-post header.

Pace is important. An accurate, driven corner is more dangerous than a 'hanging' one that takes longer to reach its target. Graham Rix is a player who has the ability to 'whip' the ball into the six-yard box with enough pace and swing to upset even the best of defenders.

Each team should have two or three other players who can take a corner-kick in case the regular corner-takers are injured.

Corner-kicking is an aspect of the game that needs constant practice. Like a golfer, the taker has to rehearse in advance. Corners are important aids to scoring. They should not be squandered.

On average there are between fifteen and twenty corners in a match, with the home side usually getting the bulk of them. The attacking team needs someone with courage to head the ball under pressure. No tactic can beat that. Courage and determination are vital factors, both for attackers and defenders.

Signalling at corners

A player taking a corner will sometimes raise an arm as a signal to colleagues waiting in the goal-area. He will have discussed this in advance with his team-mates. One arm raised might mean he is going to direct the ball towards the near post. Two arms might mean he will aim beyond the far post.

In order to confuse the opposition, this procedure will be reversed from match to match. Other teams will use other methods of signalling. Some players bounce the ball once or twice. Others will touch the corner flag.

Knowing where the ball will go gives the attacking side an advantage and makes it harder for the defenders. This is a fairly new tactic in the game.

The near-post corner

In recent years more emphasis has been put on the near-post corner because it is harder to defend against. The goalkeeper more often than not is unable to reach the ball to catch it or punch it away because he will have too many players in front of him.

The attackers at the near post can flick it on to a team-mate, running in behind them, and a goal will frequently result. The man at the near post also has the alternative of trying a glancing sideways header, which at such short range is hard to keep out.

The near-post corner is a goalkeeper's problem area.

Outswinging corner-kick

The outswinging corner is slowly coming back into fashion, and with the right players

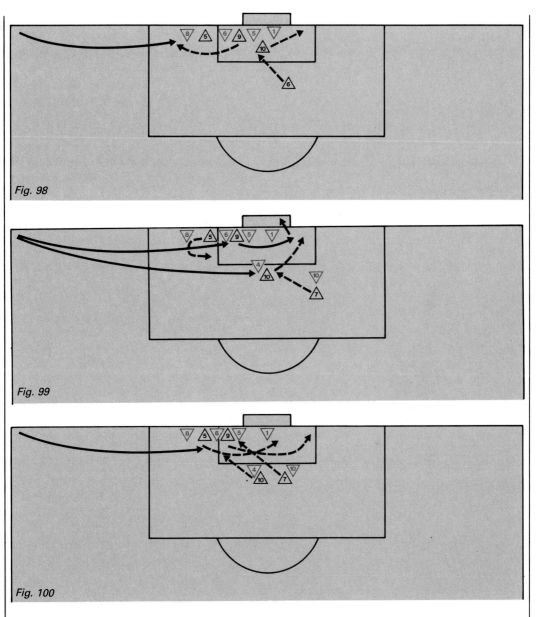

Fig. 98

Fig. 99

Fig. 100

can be just as effective as the near-post corner. The goalkeeper has to decide whether to try and catch the ball or punch it away to safety, knowing that it will be swinging away from him.

He will be less willing to go for the ball if there is a crowded box with tall centre forwards of the Mark Hateley type waiting

The near-post corner — tactics

Fig. 98 △ runs out and around the near-post group for the flick-on. △ moves back for the flick-on to the far post. △ runs in for anything central.

Fig. 99 △ goes forward, then bends out, leaving △ free for the flick-on. △ bends around the back for the flick-on. △ attacks the area in the centre of goal.

Fig. 100 △ and △ spin out to the far post for the flick-on. △ and △ run into the space they have left.

135

for it, players who can outjump their markers.

England used this type of corner very effectively in a Friendly match in Stockholm in 1986. Viv Anderson, who is a good header of the ball, lined up in a row on the edge of the six-yard box along with Terry Butcher and Alvin Martin and, as the ball came over, peeled off to the left to make his header on the far side of the box. Several times Anderson managed to evade his marker.

Variations on short corners

If the six-yard box is full of defenders, it may be advisable for the taker of the corner-kick to try an alternative, like a short pass to a nearby colleague who will then centre the ball.

Having two men on the ball at the corner-flag means that the other team have to push out two defenders from the middle to mark them, which obviously creates more space for opportunities in the danger area.

Another variation often used by Aston Villa in their European Cup days was to play the ball in along the byline for another player either to dribble closer to goal with it, if unmarked, or centre directly. Again, the idea is to draw defenders out of the middle.

Sometimes there may be an advantage in playing the ball to the edge of the penalty-

Outswinging corner-kick tactics
The light areas indicate the spaces on the far post.
Fig. 101 ▲, ▲ and ▲ stand together at the far post. ▲ and ▲ run towards the centre of goal while ▲ pulls out from the far post to get free.
Fig. 102 ▲, ▲ and ▲ stand together on the far post. ▲ darts for the near post and ▲ uses ▲ as a block to get free into the space left by ▲.
Fig. 103 ▲ stands ten yards outside the box. ▲ and ▲ run towards the centre of goal, leaving space for ▲ to come into.

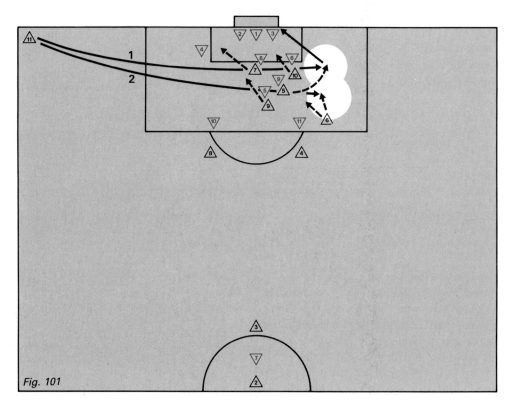

Fig. 101

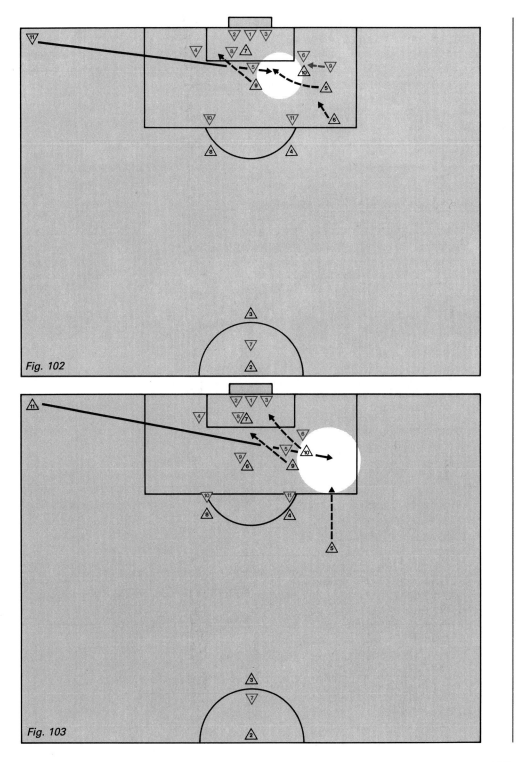

Fig. 102

Fig. 103

area for a colleague to chip across goal. In each case the corner-taker has to weigh up the situation and judge for himself which is the best course.

Often it is possible to pass the ball to the corner of the 'D', where a colleague might be free to try a shot. Terry McDermott was a player who frequently profited from this type of move, scoring goals past unsighted goalkeepers.

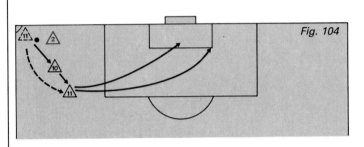

Fig. 104

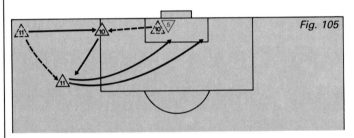

Fig. 105

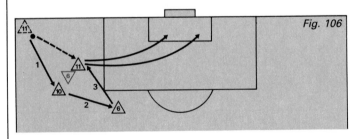

Fig. 106

Short-corner tactics

Fig. 104 The player taking the corner, ⚑, passes short to his team-mate ⚑ then overlaps him to get a better angle on goal, allowing him variation on the cross.

Fig. 105 ⚑ runs out to the kicker ⚑ to receive the ball. He then passes back to ⚑ who has moved to a better angle to cross the ball in.

Fig. 106 ⚑ passes to ⚑ who in turn passes inside to ⚑. ⚑ is now unmarked and ⚑ passes to him. Dalglish, Whelan and Souness (when he was there) used this ploy for Liverpool.

Fig. 107 There is a midfield player ⚑ unmarked on the edge of the box. ⚑ pulls the corner back to him for a volley or shot.

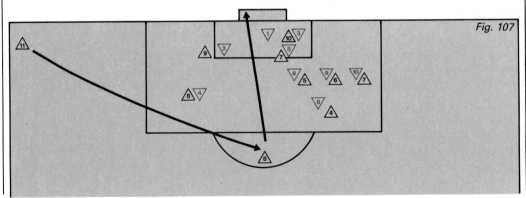

Fig. 107

Blocking the goalkeeper

Most teams will position players close to the goalkeeper to make it difficult for him to get to the ball. Leeds United were particularly adept at this in their heyday. It is perfectly legal, providing the player makes no attempt to obstruct the goalkeeper.

If the goalkeeper runs into him on his way towards the ball, it is not an infringement. The strategy of any attacking team inside the box must always be to make things difficult for the goalkeeper, within the laws of the game.

Bunching

One tactic which has been used, particularly by Watford, at corner- and free-kicks is to station players close together in a bunch. When the ball is delivered, these players break away in different directions in order to attack the ball, whatever its pace and height.

Marking at corners

There are three types of strategy: *Man-for-man* – some teams, especially Continentals, mark at corners man-for-man. *Zonal* – there are teams in England which zonal mark at corners. They station four big men on the edges of the six-yard box and three men just inside the penalty box. *A mixture of both* – in general most teams use a mixture of both systems: man-for-man marking their opponents' big dangerous players, and zonal-marking areas such as the near post and centre of goal.

Defending at corners

The goalkeeper must be the key man. If he wants a man on each post, he must have them. In the old days it was invariably the full-backs who stood on the line. But in modern football most full-backs are good in the air and therefore are wanted as markers. What often happens is that the smallest players take the posts.

A common mistake is to stand right next to the post on the line. When that happens, the defender can move only one way, towards the centre of the goal. But if he is standing a yard inside the post, he can move both ways and reduce the area left unprotected.

The defender must also be sure he does

Fig. 108 Bunching
The attacking players stand close together in the centre of goal around the penalty spot. It is very difficult for their opponents to mark them in this position. The attacking players know which way they are going to run but obviously the defenders do not.

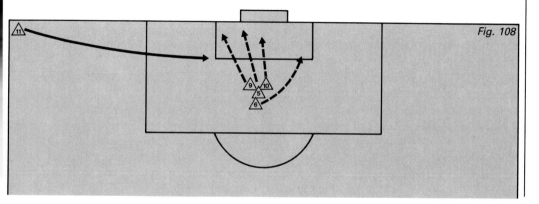

Fig. 108

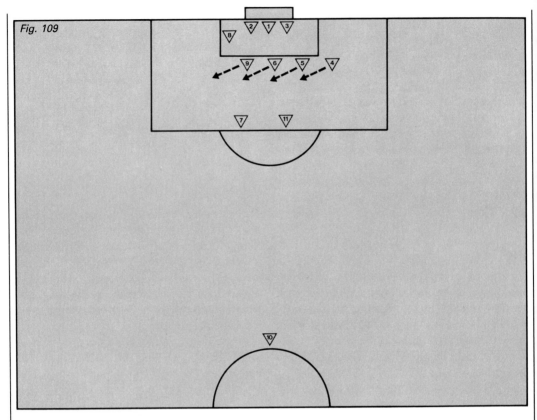

Fig. 109

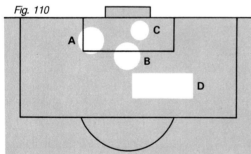

Fig. 110

Fig. 109 Zonal marking at corners
The big men ▽, ▽, ▽ and ▽ take the area just outside the six-yard box. The smaller men ▽ and ▽ mark the edge of the box. Each player must be prepared to attack the ball when it arrives in his area.

Fig. 110 Zonal and man-for-man marking at corners
The following three areas should be zonal-marked:
A The near-post zone.
B The central edge of the six-yard box.
C The flick-on zone, to prevent the opposition getting on the end of the flick.
In zone **D** the opponents' big men must be marked man-for-man.

not block the view of the goalkeeper. He should be a foot or two off the line to prevent this happening. Most managers insist on another player in the near-post area to attack the near-post corner.

Some goalkeepers will want every attacker marked, wherever he is, and each defender will have been told which player he is to pick up. But there are some goalkeepers (Liverpool's Bruce Grobbelaar is a good example) who will insist on the six-yard box being cleared of defenders because they will want to go for any ball there themselves. The coach and the goalkeeper will come to an agreement about which methods suit them and the team best.

Calling

The goalkeeper's calls at corners must be loud and clear and easily understood. If he intends to go for the ball, he must shout 'My ball, Fred!' addressing himself to the nearest defender. Not to name a player runs the risk of giving away an indirect free-kick.

If he does not intend to go for the ball, he shouts 'Away!' and once a defender clears it, the defending side must get out of the box as soon as possible to make the opponents offside.

Defenders must be alert for occasions when the goalkeeper drops the ball. They must be first to it to clear the danger. When the goalkeeper goes for the ball, the two men on the line should advance towards the centre of goal to cover him. Those defenders near the line of the ball should allow him to have a clear run at it and not get in his way.

The goalkeeper's position

This varies according to personal preference. Peter Shilton, for example, tends to go towards the near post and then backs off if he sees the ball is going deep.

The goalkeeper should be a yard off the line to give himself a good starting position. In the old days he would be stationed on the far post because more kicks would be outswingers aimed across goal. But in recent years the near-post corner has become a main attacking weapon, and goalkeepers want to put themselves in a position where they can either challenge at the near post or, if that is not possible, back off to stop the flick-on. That usually means taking up a central position.

Attackers on the half-way line

It is advisable to leave at least one or two players on the half-way line at corners, firstly to launch counter-attacks and secondly to engage the attentions of three opponents.

To leave no one up is a mistake. It merely increases the number of men to mark in the box and increases the chances of conceding a goal.

Some sides have one man on the half-way line but if there is a break, he may have difficulty retaining possession unless he has someone else to whom he can pass.

Previously the two defenders marking the lone forward would position themselves alongside him, one on either side. It has now been recognised that this makes the defenders vulnerable, so nowadays one defender puts himself in front and the other behind. The first one is there to cut out the ball before it comes to him and the second to block his run, should he get through.

Taking penalties

Penalty-taking is about confidence. The bouncy, confident player will want to take penalties, but there are not many of this type in an average side. The problem arises when the usual penalty-taker starts missing them. This happens to nearly all penalty-takers sooner or later. Some will adjust their methods and continue, others will hand the responsibility over to others.

Often in big matches no one will want to take a penalty because of the pressure. A volunteer will be needed. Each First Division side usually has two players who take penalties regularly, but if it is the last minute of a game, in front of a capacity crowd, even the strongest-hearted of players can back down.

At a Spurs v. Chelsea match, Chelsea were awarded a penalty at a crucial time and the player who asked if he could take it, former Spurs midfield player Micky Hazard, had missed two penalties against the same club two weeks earlier! Nigel Spackman, the normal penalty-taker, stood aside and Hazard duly converted from the spot. At Arsenal, Charlie Nicholas usually took the penalties, mainly because he was not frightened of missing one. He would still want to take the next one. But several misses by Nicholas led to Tony Woodcock and Brian Talbot taking over for a while before Nicholas was restored to the position.

Now that European and World Cup matches can be decided by penalties, more time is spent practising them. Sides have to prepare five players to take penalties, often saving their best takers until the end, although it is also usual to have an expert to take the first one.

It is impossible to capture the tension of the real thing in training. Nor is it easy to find as many as five penalty-takers in one team. It is often said that goalscorers are natural penalty-takers because they are used to putting the ball into the net, but this is not always the case. Some of the best penalty-takers have been full-backs, like Phil Neal when he was with Liverpool and Ray Stewart of West Ham.

There are two main ways of taking a penalty and these two players represent each style. Neal tended to place the ball inside the post with the side of his foot. Stewart blasts the ball with immense power, like his former team-mate Geoff Hurst used to in a previous West Ham side.

Stewart does not worry about direction. He knows that even if the goalkeeper manages to get a hand to the ball, the pace of it will be such that a goal will still result. Nor is he concerned if the ball is close to the goalkeeper. Most times, the goalkeeper will be diving to one side, trying to anticipate which way the ball is going.

Stewart takes a considerable run-in, starting near the extremity of the 'D'. Ronnie Allen, my former West Bromwich Albion team-mate, was one of the outstanding penalty-takers of my time and he always stressed the importance of a long run-up. He used to come up like a fast bowler and, though he preferred to place the ball, it always had plenty of pace on it.

In the Mexico World Cup many penalties were missed because players took only a few steps before trying to place the ball. There was no power in their shots and the goalkeepers were able to stop them.

The penalty-taker has to decide what he is going to do, where he is going to put the ball, and stick to it. Once he changes his mind, he can be in trouble. Only a great player like Michel Platini can watch the goalkeeper, notice which way he is committed to go and then change his mind and sidefoot the ball into the other corner of the goal.

The natural swing of the foot of a right-footed penalty-taker will take the ball to the goalkeeper's right and vice versa for a left-footed player. That is why a right-footed player will be happier to direct the ball to the right of the goalkeeper. It is natural to go across the ball instead of straight through it.

Young players are advised to aim for one of the stanchions in the back of the goal. If they can 'pass' the ball to the stanchion, few goalkeepers will be capable of keeping the ball out. These days many players are aiming for the top corners of the goal because, like the area close to the bottom of the post, it is difficult for the goalkeeper to reach that far.

Stopping Penalties

The goalkeeper is the man with nothing to lose when a penalty-kick is awarded. If he saves it, he is a hero. If he is beaten, no one minds, because players are expected to score from the spot.

So the pressure is all on the taker, not the goalkeeper. The goalkeeper can improve the odds in his favour by doing his homework. He might know where the kicker normally places his penalties. In League football, spies always make notes of such points and pass them on to their own goalkeeper.

If the goalkeeper knows a player always puts the ball to his right, he will move a foot or two that way instead of remaining in the centre of the goal. This will put extra pressure on the taker. It might make him opt to do something he does not like doing, i.e. aiming for the other side.

Anticipation is the key. If the goalkeeper can decide which way the ball is going in advance, he is half-way to saving it. I advise goalkeepers to look at the eyes of the taker. Often, the man approaching the ball will look in the direction where he intends to place it.

If he knows the taker likes to blast the ball, the goalkeeper should stand up and not move until the foot makes contact with the ball. That way he gives himself more chance of getting a hand to the ball which may pass close to him. But what usually happens is that the goalkeeper is diving either to his right or left and the ball whistles past him high in the centre of goal.

It is difficult to tell a goalkeeper to stand up and not try to anticipate. If he stands there and the ball is hit powerfully into the corner, people will say, 'Why didn't he move?' Some goalkeepers try to narrow the angle by stepping forward and diving, but that is illegal.

Saving penalties requires lightning reflexes and it also requires a good memory. One of the best goalkeepers for stopping penalties for many years in England was Paul Cooper when he was at Ipswich. He was a player who did his homework.

The most difficult thing for a goalkeeper, once he has blocked the shot, is to smother the rebound. The pace of the ball usually takes it back towards the onrushing penalty-taker, and the odds are very much against him making a second stop.

This is where team planning comes in. The defending side has to be sure to station defenders on the edge of the 'D', so they are in pole position to rush in and try to clear the ball. The other team will want to station their men in the same position, which is why so much pushing and shoving goes on at penalties.

The referee, who usually stands alongside the penalty-spot, frequently fails to see this jostling and has to rely on his linesman. I believe the referee should stand further back, inside the 'D', so that he can see not only if a goalkeeper moves before the ball is kicked but also if players of either side encroach, as they often do.

Most referees will look at the goalkeeper and wait for the sound of the ball being kicked. It is hard to see both, but by being further back they would give themselves a better opportunity of spotting infringements. Many penalty-kicks should be retaken because a goalkeeper moves or there is encroachment, but it seldom happens.

Goalkeeping

A good goalkeeper is worth twenty points a season to his team.

Goalkeeper is the thinking man's position. During a game the goalkeeper constantly has to make decisions and his judgement must be right.

In many ways he is the most important man in the team, because if he makes a mistake, he can cost his side the game. But I do not subscribe to the idea that the goalkeeper should be considered apart and should train solely on his own.

A goalkeeper's training should be divided into two parts:

1 *Individual* – reaction work, agility exercises and technique work.

2 *Team work* – working with his back-four for understanding and familiarity. Catching crosses, calling and practical shot stopping.

The goalkeeper is part of a team and has to work with his defenders. He has to read the game from his vantage point at the rear, and organise the players in front of him. He also has to act as a sweeper when the ball is played behind the back-four, and that demands speed, fitness and sound judgement. He must be continually talking to and advising the rest of the team.

When he gets the ball, his distribution must be good. A poor clearance can give the ball away and lead to a goal. This part of the game has improved tremendously in recent years. Few professional goalkeepers are now inadequate distributors.

Most clubs now have a goalkeeping coach. The England squad has one in Mike Kelly; Bob Wilson fills the role at Arsenal and Spurs, Peter Bonetti at Chelsea, and specialist goalkeeping coaches, like Gordon Banks and Alan Hodgkinson, visit a number of clubs.

In schools there is a tendency to give the goalkeeper's jersey to a big lad who cannot run. That, of course, is nonsense. The task should be given to the boy who is best suited to do the job and more important, the boy who *wants* to do it. The candidate must have a good pair of hands – be able to catch the ball and hold on to it – and be prepared to throw himself about. A boy who lacks agility and does not like diving should not be considered.

A poor goalkeeper can cost a team the game. A good one can inspire victory. His primary duty is to stop the ball entering the net, and to be successful his game needs to be based on a sound technique. To be a top-class goalkeeper requires a tremendous amount of hard work. No one works harder in the England set-up than Peter Shilton, a man whose professionalism is renowned throughout the world.

The Goalkeeper's Physique

All the best goalkeepers – Frank Swift, Lev Yachin, Bert Williams, Gordon Banks, Sepp Maier, Dino Zoff, Ray Clemence and Peter Shilton – have been around six feet tall. That is the ideal height. There have been smaller goalkeepers who reached International class, like Alan Hodgkinson, Eddie Hopkinson and Ron Springett, but they are exceptions. To be inordinately tall, say six feet six inches, is a disadvantage.

Players of that height have difficulty in getting down to low shots.

The best weight for a goalkeeper is between thirteen and fourteen stone, which is heavier than an outfield player. Goalkeepers need a powerful physique to withstand challenges in the air. They need to 'fill the goal'.

The most demanding part of a goalkeeper's job is continually getting up after he has dived to the ground. To do that requires strength of an exceptional nature. When Shilton is training with England, Mike Kelly will be giving him pressure training which requires him to keep going down for the ball, and getting up, hundreds of times.

Fitness

It is a common misconception that a goalkeeper needs only to practise stopping shots and crosses. Nowadays, his physical preparation must be as good as that of any outfield player. He has to join in the sprints and also the stamina work. In addition to that, he should use weights to strengthen his wrists, arms and shoulders, and to develop his thighs for jumping.

Mental Attitude

The mental demands on the goalkeeper are far greater than those made on any other player. He has to be constantly alert, adjusting his position to meet any danger. There will be long periods when he is not called upon, but he must not let his mind wander. He needs one hundred per cent concentration all the time.

The goalkeeper who simply stands there is the one who is usually caught out. Good goalkeepers will be continually on the move, patrolling the edge of the box when play is at the other end and adapting their position to be ready to make a save when their goal is threatened.

They will be talking all the time to the players in front of them because the goalkeepers' panoramic view of the pitch enables them to see the problems building up for defenders. They have to work hard at shouting. I have seen some goalkeepers practically hoarse after a match.

A goalkeeper has to be able to accept criticism. As the most exposed player in the team, his mistakes will be analysed, whereas the mistakes of outfield players will probably be subjected to much less attention.

If he is beaten, he must say to himself, 'How did I let that one in?' His technique may be at fault, his angle might have been wrong, or his timing coming off the line remiss. Most professional clubs video their matches, so that modern goalkeepers can assess where they went wrong, work at it in training and put it right with the help of their specialist coach.

Sweeping

A new technique for goalkeepers has emerged in recent years. It is called 'sweeping'.

With most defences moving up towards the half-way line as soon as possible, a large space is created behind them and opposing teams will try to play the ball into that space to enable a forward to break through unattended.

In the early days of goalkeeping, the keeper was expected to stay on his line and stop shots. Then his role evolved into a wider-ranging one which required him to dominate his goal-area and go for the ball whenever it approached that area. More recently he has been expected to dominate not just the goal area but the whole of the penalty-area.

145

Bruce Grobbelaar of Liverpool will frequently come to the edge of the penalty-area, not merely to intercept through-passes but to take crosses as well. His predecessor, Ray Clemence, was one of the first to master the skill of 'sweeping', or coming outside the penalty-area to clear the ball before a forward could reach it. The Dutch used this technique as part of their 'total' football in the 1974 World Cup with Jan Jongbloed, their unathletic-looking goalkeeper, playing an important part.

Fig. 111 Sweeping behind the defence
This diagram shows where the goalkeeper should be standing when he is sweeping behind his back-four. He should position himself in the penalty area in the corresponding section to where the ball is in play on the pitch: if the ball is in area 3 of the pitch the goalkeeper should be in area 3 of the box, if the ball is in area 2 of the pitch the goalkeeper should be in area 2 of the box, and so on.

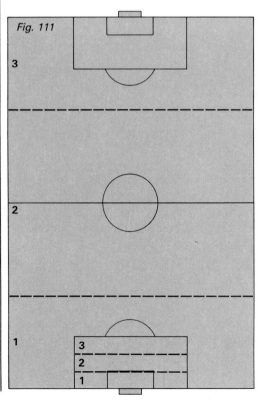

The three essential requirements of a goalkeeper in this role are:

1 A good starting position.

2 Good reading of the game to spot the through-ball early.

3 Good pace and sprinting ability.

When he is well outside the box, the goalkeeper cannot use his hands. If he tries to kick the ball hurriedly, he risks slicing it or missing it altogether. His aim must be to ensure that he kicks the ball cleanly, deep into the opponents' half or over the safety of the touch-line.

There are occasions, if the ball is bouncing, when he might have to head it away. That obviously requires good timing and a reasonable ability to head the ball!

The Goalkeeping Free-Kick

Another more recent innovation is the free-kick taken by the goalkeeper outside the penalty-area. Dave Beasant of Wimbledon was one of the first goalkeepers to use this idea.

It enables the defenders to move right up to the half-way line, taking their opponents that much further away from their own goal. It also allows the ten outfield players to push up into the opponents' half, ready to win the knock-down and attack from there. But if the goalkeeper miscues and makes a poor kick, he can be in trouble.

Equipment

In the past, goalkeepers would only wear gloves when the ball was wet. Today, most goalkeepers wear them in all conditions, wet or dry. The design of gloves has improved so much that they are a valuable aid to any

(*Left*) West Germany's long-serving goalkeeper Sepp Maier was one of the first to make a habit of using specially designed gloves. He also set a trend by wearing longer shorts to keep the thighs warm.

goalkeeper, whatever class of football he is playing in.

The biggest influence on the subject of gloves was the West German goalkeeper Sepp Maier. He used huge, rubberised gloves with pimpled rubber grips and soon goalkeepers all over the world were copying him. Some designs even have sticky surfaces!

Wearing gloves will not make you a better goalkeeper, but it will help on occasions when catching the ball, particularly if it is raining. Nevertheless, I always insist that my goalkeepers have two training sessions a week without gloves, so they can get a feel of the ball and their hands will harden.

Most goalkeepers prefer to wear shorts which are tight around the thighs and longer than those worn by outfield players. Maier's were almost down to his knees. Longer shorts give extra protection to the thighs and provide warmth. Warmth is important to goalkeepers, especially when they are in-active. Their pre-match warm-up should be long enough and hard enough to give them a gentle sweat, and they will want to maintain this.

On harder pitches, especially on artificial surfaces, goalkeepers will wear tracksuit bottoms with padded knees and hips. They will also have elbow padding to prevent 'burns'.

A cap with a large peak will be part of the vital equipment needed by the goalkeeper, more so on a hot, sunny day. Caps used today are lightweight and tight-fitting, not easily knocked off.

Goalkeepers' jerseys used to be restricted to four primary colours, the most common colour being green. In recent years the rule has been relaxed and it is now possible to wear multi-coloured shirts which are easier to see, especially on television. But the choice of colours has to be different from the strip used by the outfield players of both sides.

Shin-pads are used by many goalkeepers, though some prefer not to use them despite the fact there is always the risk of collisions which can cause cuts and bruises.

The choice of boot will depend on the conditions. If the pitch is soft, the boot should have a longer stud, as with an out-field player. However, the goal-mouth wears out the quickest, so it is important that the goalkeeper inspects the goal-area himself. It will be different from the rest of the pitch, either harder or softer, especially on frosty grounds when the goal-mouth has been protected.

Injuries to Goalkeepers

Surprisingly, in view of the hazardous nature of their work, goalkeepers do not sustain as many, or as serious, injuries as outfield players.

Most of the records for the greatest number of appearances have been set by goalkeepers. Pat Jennings and Ray Clemence were two record-breakers, and they did not have many bad injuries in their long careers.

Equally surprising, not many goal-keepers break their fingers through stopping, or trying to stop, the ball. The most vulner-able finger is the little finger and the injury usually happens when a low shot is being saved and the finger stubs into the ground. Some goalkeepers tape their third and fourth fingers together to prevent this happening.

Collisions are fairly infrequent and if they do happen, the outfield player usually comes off worse than the goalkeeper. Facial injuries can be sustained by elbows, but probably the most serious injury a goalkeeper can suffer is to his head when diving to take the ball from the feet of a forward.

The most common injury is a cut or a broken nose. Bravery is clearly an asset for any goalkeeper, but a good technique, and making the save at the right time, can eliminate most of the risks.

Shot-Stopping

Starting position

The feet should be shoulder-width apart, with the weight on the balls of the feet. The arms should be slightly outside the line of the body with the hands in a ready position. The legs should be flexed to give a solid base, providing a good, pushing-off position. The head should be still and tilting slightly forward.

Ground shots – straight at the goalkeeper

There are two ways to stop a ground shot straight at the goalkeeper. The first is the stopping technique. The legs are moved into line with the shot and kept close enough to prevent the ball passing through. The hands go down, palms facing the ball, and the ball is scooped up towards the chest. The head should remain steady and the eyes should be directed at the ball as long as possible.

The advantage of this technique is that if the ball suddenly wobbles and is diverted, the goalkeeper is in a good position to adjust. With the second method, the kneeling technique, the goalkeeper has less chance to change his position. On a bumpy pitch the ball could hit a divot and fly over the goalkeeper's shoulder into the net.

The kneeling technique demands that the feet and lower body should be sideways-on to the ball, giving a wider area to defend. The knee of the kneeling leg should be level with the inside of the heel of the other leg. The palms should be facing the ball ready to scoop it to safety in the arms. The head should remain still.

Ground shot to the side (diving)

The starting position will be as already outlined. The throwing of the body into the

(Below) The starting position.

(Overleaf) Diving and holding a low shot.

line of the ball must be timed right, with the weight on the leg nearer to the direction of the ball, which will propel the body. The bottom hand will get behind the ball, with the other hand following and landing on top of it. The body should follow the hands and get behind the ball. It is important that the goalkeeper has a clear vision of the ball, unobstructed by either arm.

Ground shot close to the body (collapsing save)

The hard, low shot which passes close to the body is often one of the most difficult to stop. Many watchers do not appreciate that. They will applaud a relatively easy save at a comfortable height and ignore the skill involved when the goalkeeper manages to block a shot a foot or two away from him.

The goalkeeper must get his feet out of the way quickly, allowing the top half of his

(*Above and right*) Knocking the ball around the post.

body to get down. According to the time he has, he will either put one hand or both hands on to the ball.

As it is a quick, reaction save, all he has time to do is knock the ball away or round a post.

Use of the feet for the ground shot close to the body

The use of the feet can often get the goalkeeper out of trouble. To jab out a foot to knock the ball away is often as much as a goalkeeper can expect to do, and can be just as effective as using his hands (*Fig. 112* on page 155).

Bob Wilson used to spend a lot of time with Pat Jennings and John Lukic at Arsenal, getting them to use their feet in this situation.

Waist-high shots straight at the goalkeeper

The feet should be about shoulder-width apart, knees flexed in a good balanced position. The hands should be facing the ball and the head kept still. The ball should be cradled firmly into the abdomen, the top half of the body leaning slightly forwards over the ball.

Chest-high shots at the goalkeeper

The positioning should be the same and the ball should be trapped against the chest and held firmly. Some goalkeepers (Pat Jennings was one) prefer to knock a powerful shot down to the ground, taking the pace out of it and catching the rebound. The aim must be to gain possession of the ball at the first opportunity.

Head-high shots – or higher

Using the same starting position, the fingers will be stretching upwards to catch the ball. The fingers must be firm but not too rigid, otherwise the ball could easily be dropped. The thumbs will be close together at the rear of the ball to stop it slipping through the hands. Having caught the ball, the goalkeeper brings it down on to his chest, hugging his hands and arms over it for safety.

Depending on the pace and height of the ball, the goalkeeper might decide to turn it over the crossbar. If it is a hard shot, he will deflect the ball up and over the bar with the palm or palms, making sure it is well above the bar. Some goalkeepers do this with the back of the hand, helping the ball on its way, but I do not recommend this practice.

Angles

Getting the angles right is all-important to a goalkeeper. Every time the angle from

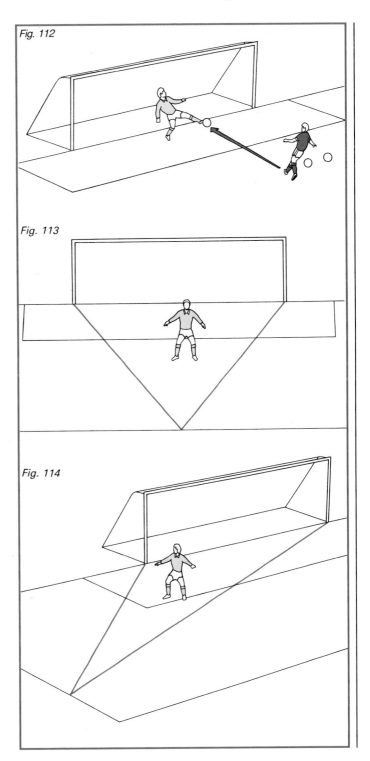

Fig. 112

Fig. 113

Fig. 114

(*Above*) Catching a chest-high shot.

which the ball is coming changes, so he must adjust his position. In training, I advise using ropes as a guide.

For example, if the ball is in the centre of the penalty-area, the ropes will lead from the ball to the two posts, and the goalkeeper knows he has to be in the middle of the triangle and as far out as possible from his line (*Fig. 113*).

If the line of attack is from the side, the ropes have to be shifted, and the goalkeeper takes up a position midway between them, getting as far out as he can (*Fig. 114*). He will need to

move slightly to the near post to cover his vulnerable spot. It is a rule of goalkeeping that, wherever possible, the goalkeeper should not be beaten on his near post.

Most goalkeepers reach out and touch the near post to get their position right. They do it for two reasons:

1 To make sure they are not too close or too far away from the near post.

2 If they touch it and then move forward a few inches, they know that, should they have to dive at the near post for a shot, they will not collide with it because they are standing outside the line of the post.

The goalkeeper will adjust to a similar position when the threat is from the other side. The movement of the feet should be such that he is in a balanced position to make a save. Jumping should be avoided and so should the crossing of legs.

Marking the pitch is a cautionable offence,

so the goalkeeper has to judge his angles from the penalty-spot and the markings of the perimeter of the goal-area. Practising in a proper goal with proper markings is essential for positional play.

How far should the goalkeeper come off his line? That must be for him to decide but he must remember that, if he comes out too far, he runs the risk of seeing the ball lobbed or chipped over his head.

The essentials of narrowing the angle are:

1 Short steps while advancing, so as to be always ready to make the save.

2 An upright and alert body position. Hands low down at the side.

3 The goalkeeper has to make himself look 'big', presenting as large an obstacle as possible.

4 He has to out-think the shooter, perhaps kidding him by showing a bit more of one side than the other.

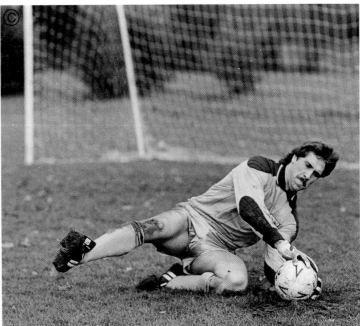

5 He must adjust his position to counter the angle of the projected shot and he must be prepared to attack the shot.

(*Above*) Spreading.

Outwitting the Opponent

If the goalkeeper positions himself right, he can take the initiative and make the first move. He can pretend to go one way by moving an arm and motioning as though he is anticipating a shot to one side, while still maintaining his upright position.

This is called 'dummying' your opponent. Forwards do it all the time but there is no reason why the goalkeeper should not also try it. His opponent will see the movement out of the top corner of his eye and might react to it.

In a one-against-one situation, the goalkeeper can make the odds favour him if he makes a positive move. But first he must hold his position. To come racing out and try to fling himself at the ball, unless it has run beyond the control of the forward, is foolhardy. By holding his position and covering his angles, he creates doubt in the mind of the forward and is on the way to winning the duel between them.

Spreading

There will be occasions when it is not possible to 'hold', and the goalkeeper has to spread his body in such a way as to block the shot. This must really be the last resort because the ball will rebound off the goalkeeper and there is a risk that another forward will be first to it and a goal could result.

The timing must be right. If the goalkeeper goes too early, an intelligent forward like

157

Brian McClair or Clive Allen will lift the ball over his body.

The technique of spreading requires:

1 Getting the body low and horizontal, leading with the hands. The idea is to block the shot with any part of the body.

2 Attacking the player on the ball quickly, making him rush his shot. If he gets his shot in but it goes wide, you have won the duel.

3 Expecting him to go one way, let the hands and arms cover that. Then should he go the other way, the bottom half of your body covers that by sweeping round with your legs and feet.

Neville Southall of Everton and Wales is a terrific exponent of this type of save, and any young goalkeeper will learn a lot by watching him.

(*Above*) Liverpool goalkeeper Bruce Grobbelaar shows the bravery that is needed to dive head first to gain possession of the ball while a forward (Paul Mariner) is challenging.

Catching Crosses

Catching the ball when it is in the air and crossed from a wide position is undoubtedly the hardest part of the goalkeeper's job. It requires judgement, bravery, a sound technique and a good pair of hands.

Because the ball is in the air so much in British football, our goalkeepers are probably better than most in this department. Once the goalkeeper decides to go for the ball, he must see it through. Many goals scored in this situation result from the goalkeeper starting to move, then changing his mind and getting caught out of position. The best he can then hope for is that a defender will head the ball away.

A goalkeeper who handles crosses confidently and dominates the six-yard box gives a tremendous lift to his colleagues. One who evades his responsibilities unnerves those around him.

There are so many different kinds of crosses for the goalkeeper to deal with, from hard-driven ones to those that hang in the air (the most difficult), from ones that swing away from him to ones that swing in (almost as difficult), from ones that swerve or dip to those that are mis-hit, and so on.

Starting position

When the ball comes from a wide position, the goalkeeper can be well off his line in the central part of the goal because he has time to back off or advance. But when the ball is brought closer to his goal, he has to cover his near post more. He then puts himself at risk against a chipped cross to the far post and depends on defenders to cover him.

The essential points of catching a cross are:

1 The goalkeeper must half-face the direction of the ball in an angled position so that he can see the ball and outfield players.

2 Once he decides to go, he must keep his eyes on the ball. In a crowded goal-area this is hard to do, but he must not be distracted.

3 A call should be made quickly and firmly – 'My ball, Bobby!' – to warn colleagues.

4 Judgement of the pace and flight of the ball has to be precise.

5 The goalkeeper has to be certain that there is a route out for him towards the path of the ball. If he is hemmed in and decides not to go, he has to let his colleagues know by shouting – 'Away, John!'.

6 Lift-off comes from strong legs, hence the need for specialised training. He needs to work at a good, strong spring from a one-footed take-off.

7 The goalkeeper must aim to take the ball at its highest point. He will be able to reach higher than any forward can reach with his head.

8 Invariably, he will be challenged and must be strong enough to resist a bump in the air. If he is not, he will drop the ball.

9 The goalkeeper must catch the ball and bring it into the safe custody of the chest, looking for a quick kick or throw out.

10 When going for a 'hanging' cross, it is advisable for him to delay and get the timing right. Too early and he risks getting under the ball and being jostled off it. Not all referees will penalise attackers when a goalkeeper collides with someone!

Catching a high far-post cross

A similar technique is employed with short backward steps to cover ground and get in position. As the body will be off-balance when the ball is caught, making sure he holds on to the ball is vital if he falls to the ground. He must not let the impact with the turf jolt the ball out of his hands.

Knee up

When the goalkeeper comes for a cross, he will spring off one leg and usually have the other one raised, knee first. It is a natural movement and no referee will penalise him if contact is made with an opponent.

But if he straightens his leg to deter a challenge, that is a different matter. It is dangerous play and will be punished.

Punching

(*Above*) Catching a cross.

(*Right*) Two-fisted punching.

Catching the ball is preferable to punching, but there are occasions in packed goal-mouths when it is impossible for the goal-keeper to catch the ball. His aim then must be to punch the ball in such a way that it travels a fair distance away from the danger area.

The essentials are the same – early judge-ment, a positive move towards the ball, an attempt to meet the ball at the highest point and closest distance from the touch-line.

Should he use one fist or two? That must be up to the goalkeeper. The general rule is that, if possible, he should use both fists to get the maximum possible contact with the ball.

There are two ways to punch the ball:

1 The fists close together, with thumbs touching and the second joints of the fingers touching. The arms should be bent and the aim should be to give the ball a short, sharp upward punch (*Fig. 115*).

Fig. 115

2 It is rare, however, that the two-fisted punch is used in modern football. Mostly the goalkeeper finds that he is only able to get one fist to the ball, which increases the risk of not timing the interception properly, or missing the ball altogether.

Deflecting the Ball with One Hand

There are times when the goalkeeper cannot punch or catch the ball, but under pressure has to turn it away with one hand. An open palm, as he falls backwards, will be enough to help the ball on out of the path of an opponent; but should the goalkeeper fall he has to be instantly back on his feet and facing the danger.

The other deflection save is when the goalkeeper is under challenge and the ball is under the crossbar. Instead of catching or punching, he may want to take the safety-first way out and push the ball over the bar with his palm and fingers. If possible, the ball should be contacted when it is above the bar.

Some goalkeepers use the back of the hand to divert the ball, but that is not to be recommended.

Blocking an Opponent to Protect the Goalkeeper

When the goalkeeper gives an early shout for the ball and goes for it, his colleagues can help him by clearing a path and thwarting any challenges. Defenders can make it easier for him by stationing themselves in a position where they can block a forward going to meet the goalkeeper as he reaches for the ball.

This is perfectly legal as long as the defender does not try to thrust himself in the way of his opponent.

Distribution

Stopping the ball from entering the net and holding crosses are the defensive side of the goalkeeper's job. The attacking side is what he does with the ball when he has possession.

Distributing the ball, either by kicking or throwing it, is just as important as shot-stopping. If the goalkeeper constantly gives the ball away, he undoes all the good work he has done earlier.

If he cannot kick the ball out of his own half, his team risks being penned in there. Too many goalkeepers find it hard to kick the ball properly but that can be corrected by practice and dedication.

When I worked with Pat Jennings at Arsenal, I used to get him to kick the ball into areas where he could do the most damage e.g. at defenders in the opposing team who were poor in the air. If a centre-half is good at heading the ball huge distances, it makes little sense to kick the ball in his direction. Over the years Pat became one of the longest kickers in the game, once scoring a goal direct from a drop-kick.

A quickly-taken clearance to a colleague can turn defence into attack and catch the opposition when they are most vulnerable. But accuracy is essential, otherwise it keeps the other team on the attack.

The goalkeeper's vision on kicking or throwing

Once a goalkeeper is in possession of the ball, he should be thinking 'counter-attack' immediately.

His first look should be downfield at his forwards, searching for 1 *v.* 1 or 2 *v.* 2 situations on the half-way line. He should then kick a good, accurate high ball to take advantage.

Having kicked the ball, he should shout 'Out!', getting his defenders upfield to sup-

(*Left*) Deflecting the ball with one hand.

port the attack and take pressure off his goal.

More times than not, his best throw-out route is to change the play. For example, he might get possession from the left and throw out to the right, and vice versa.

Work should be done in training to get understanding and method into this move.

Goal-kicks

Unless he is injured, the goalkeeper should take all the goal-kicks. If another player takes them, it enables the opposition to push up on goal, putting pressure on the defending team.

Four, five or six short steps, with the approach at a slight angle, should be sufficient to gain the necessary distance from the kick, which should be to the half-way line or beyond. Some present-day goalkeepers can reach well over the half-way line.

Good distance and accuracy are impossible if the approach is straight-on. It has to be from an angle. The head should be kept down, eyes on the ball with the non-kicking

(*Above*) Kicking from the hands.

leg alongside and close to the ball. The ankle must be firm with toe down, laces into the ball, and the leg should follow through.

Kicking from the hands

Kicking from the hands is much easier than kicking from a stationary position on the ground, and the distance achieved is far greater. Using this method, many goalkeepers can kick up to and around the opposing penalty-area. The same principles apply – eyes on the ball, clean kick and a meaningful follow-through.

Some goalkeepers throw the ball up a little before kicking it. As David Seaman shows, the best course is to drop the ball on to the kick, so it is in the air for the minimum amount of time.

The higher the kick, the better (without losing distance). Balls dropping from a good height are difficult for the opposing defenders to deal with.

The half-volley kick

The same procedure is adopted, but the ball is kicked as it contacts the ground. It is possible to achieve a good distance from a lower trajectory and it is an effective way of finding a forward quickly, especially into the wind. But the margin of error is small. The ball can bounce awkwardly and the kick can be hooked or sliced.

Kicking with both feet

It is important that goalkeepers are able to kick with both feet. If not, opponents will sometimes detail a forward to 'stand' on the goalkeeper, forcing him to use his bad foot when clearing the ball. This practice is less widespread these days because the forward may be caught offside.

A goalkeeper who is one-footed can overcome the problem by feinting a move one way and then going the other, or by throwing the ball to a colleague. But ideally the goalkeeper wants his defenders upfield, not on the edge of the box.

The four-step law

Since the four-step law was brought in, goalkeepers can parry or push the ball with their hands to the ground instead of holding it. This gives them the opportunity of advancing and dribbling the ball forwards before kicking or throwing it out.

Throwing the ball

Up to forty or so yards, it is quicker and easier for the goalkeeper to find a colleague with his throw. Over that distance it is easier to obtain accuracy. The goalkeeper should aim to be a good distributor of the ball and, whether by kicking or throwing, he should make certain that the ball is used to the benefit of his team.

The chief ways of throwing the ball are:

1 *Under-arm* – Up to twenty yards, it is possible to gain maximum accuracy with a throw similar to the action of a bowls player. The ball is released along the ground from a position level with the front foot. The advantage for the receiver is that he does

(*Top*) Throwing the ball underarm.

(*Above*) Throwing the ball overarm in a bowling action to achieve more distance.

not have a problem controlling the ball, which reaches him like a normal ground pass.

2 *Over-arm* – The action is similar to bowling in cricket, with the body sideways-

on, legs wide apart to ensure balance and arm rotating in a sling action. The advantage of this type of throw is that it is possible to get greater distance (up to forty yards) and more pace.

3 *The push* – The action here is similar to putting the shot in athletics. The ball is held at shoulder-height in the palm of the hand. The elbow is bent, the body face-on, and the ball is propelled by the extending of the

(*Above*) The push-throw.

arm. The ball is released quickly and, with a low trajectory, it is possible to mount a quick counter-attack.

4 *The backward-spinning push-throw* – This is a variation of the push-throw used by more experienced goalkeepers. They hold the hand under the bottom half of the ball and impart back-spin to slow it down. Pat Jennings used a similar throw with a flinging motion of the arm, almost parallel to the ground.

Calling

Once the throw has been made, the goal-keeper's job is not finished. He should be telling the receiver what to do with the ball. Either to 'hold', or play it back. A good goalkeeper is in constant touch with the players around him.

Throwing – the main points

1 Accuracy.

2 Not too hard (hard to control).
Not too slow (opponent closes down).

3 Hit the floor well in front of the receiver, so that the ball slides along the ground, making it easy to deal with.

4 Find a man in a space who can go forward (good reading of the game).

168

III
Fitness and Training

The Importance of Fitness

'Work-rate' has become a derided term in some parts of the game. Some critics will criticise coaches who talk about work-rate, saying, 'Let's get back to the skills of the game.'

They are wrong. If it is all about skill, why do players have to retire in their early thirties? They have to retire because their fitness goes and they cannot keep up with the running. Their skills may be at their peak but their legs have gone.

To compensate for the deterioration in the body, the thickening of legs and torso, and the loss of elasticity and pace, players have to train harder the older they get, not less hard.

If the respective skills of two sides are equal, the contest will be decided by fitness. The team that will win is the one that can indulge its skills right to the ninetieth minute. To dribble requires a high standard of fitness, to support players off the ball requires a similarly high standard and to defend for long periods also demands fitness.

If you ask a professional player: 'When do you feel at your best?' He will reply: 'When I am in good condition.' He will not deny that he plays better when he is at maximum fitness.

Until the age of around twenty-four, most players have natural fitness, but they still have to train hard to obtain the best possible results. After twenty-four, training becomes less easy. Some players will want to train by themselves to top up the training they have at their clubs. These are the dedicated types who will last longer in the game.

In a normal week most clubs will have one day when they work their players extremely rigorously with conditioning sessions.

Usually at professional clubs it is a Tuesday. The coach will often find himself unpopular as he urges his players to greater efforts. Frequently players will shout and complain at him but they all know it is for their own good. I never worry about the moaning. In the bath afterwards the player has a sense of achievement. It will give him an inner strength to know that he is likely to be fitter than his opponents.

Professionals soon lose respect for coaches who do not keep good discipline in training. If players cheat in training, or are allowed to get away with lax habits, they will cheat in matches and not work as hard as they should. That is a recipe for disaster. It is the way to lose matches.

Some of the most gifted players have found it hard to train. They enjoyed playing but were less enamoured of condition sessions, sprinting and other work which had to be put in on the training pitch. It was not a coincidence that these players retired at a comparatively early age.

Modern systems of play require good fitness. The Dutch version of 'total' football in the Seventies, for example, required players to make lots of runs off the ball all over the pitch for the whole game.

The most successful teams have always been the fittest. No team was fitter than the Wolverhampton Wanderers side, managed by Stan Cullis in the Fifties, or the Arsenal and Tottenham 'Double' sides. Liverpool trained hard in the days of the late Bill Shankly and still spend plenty of time out on the pitch, despite the high number of matches their success forces them to play each season.

The real test of English football is to last

the ten-month season and maintain fitness until the end. No club does that better than Liverpool.

Fitness also requires a responsible life off the pitch – not too much drinking and a proper, controlled diet.

The Football League season lasts ten months. 'It's not a sprint, it's a marathon', said the late Bill Shankly.

Injuries

In a body-contact sport like football, injuries are inevitable. But ensuring a high level of fitness and undertaking proper warm-up exercises before games can minimise the risk of being sidelined.

Footballing injuries range from minor strains to broken legs. Each season in the Football League, five per cent of the players are forced to retired through injury. With the right diagnosis and treatment, it is often possible to prolong an injured player's career, but sadly in amateur football it is difficult to obtain either.

Not all the ninety-two Football League clubs have a fully qualified physiotherapist. The Professional Footballers' Association revealed in 1986–7 that no less than twenty-nine clubs lacked a qualified person.

Consequently many matches take place without such a person in attendance. One way of remedying that is for the manager, coach or someone else connected with the club to take the FA's three-week training course and learn the rudimentaries.

After a player has strained a muscle, it is helpful if he can start a programme of stretching exercises in the early stages of the recovery period. This helps him to regain mobility and enables him to begin playing again more quickly than he would normally. But he needs expert advice.

Anti-inflammation tablets are now more commonly used and there is no harm in taking them because they aid a quick recovery. Ice is also an essential at any game, whether it is at Wembley or on a park pitch. These days it should be possible for every team to have a supply readily available.

The application of ice which is wrapped in a towel or cloth (to apply it straight on to the skin can cause burns) slows down the bleeding process in the case of a bad bruise and should be continued later under a pressure bandage. Such treatment speeds recovery. More serious injuries like deep cuts and breaks should obviously be treated in hospital.

The increase in the number of artificial pitches in the League is not welcomed by the players, who find they collect more injuries, besides risking long-term joint damage. A common injury is the 'burned' skin which a player suffers when falling. Unlike grass burns, these can take up to a month to heal.

The following is a brief outline of some common injuries and simple methods of treatment. With more serious injuries, the player must see his doctor or attend a hospital.

Abrasions

Players can suffer grazes or minor cuts at any time, particularly early and late in the season. It is imperative to clean the wound with antiseptic, and although it may be necessary to cover the affected area, exposure to the air will aid the healing process. More serious cuts require expert medical attention.

Blisters

Blisters are prevalent when the ground is hard and players are advised to reduce the chances of getting them by rubbing soft soap or vaseline on the inside of their socks.

This cuts down on the friction that causes the blisters.

Blisters soon clear up, but if it is necessary to lance a troublesome one, the needle should be sterilised and the area protected by a dry, clean dressing.

Athlete's Foot and Ingrowing Toenails

Athlete's foot is caused by wearing tight boots and should be treated with a powder obtainable from most chemists. In severe cases the patient should go to a chiropodist.

Proper treatment of the feet is very important. Many players do not bother to cut their toenails properly and are surprised when they suffer from ingrowing toenails. Toenails should be cut straight across, not in a rounded fashion. The feet are the tools of the footballer. They should be treated with care and respect. And they should be kept clean!

Bruising

Bruises result from blows which damage soft tissues, blood vessels, muscle sheaths and fibres. The best treatment is the application of ice or cold compresses and pressure bandages to reduce the swelling. With deep-seated bruising, like a haematoma, which is fairly common among footballers and is usually suffered on the thigh, expert physiotherapy is usually necessary. Gentle stretching exercises are helpful.

Cramp

Cramp comes from fatigue and fatigue comes from lack of fitness. Some experts recommend that players who suffer from cramp should take more salt but I say they should train harder!

The affected muscle is usually the calf muscle, and the treatment is to lie down and stretch it by straightening the leg with the toes raised and the heel pressed down. Some players believe cramp is brought on by wearing tie-ups too tight, so they take them off and play with their socks around their ankles. This is a fallacy and to play without protection is an invitation to further injury.

Achilles Tendon

With so much twisting, turning and stopping in the modern game, and tackles from behind, the Achilles tendon has become a vulnerable area. More players are needing operations to cure problems associated with the tendon. Stretching exercises can help, but in the case of a more serious, long-term injury, medical advice must be sought. Some players with sore Achilles tendons wear a pad in the heel of their shoe in normal life. It lifts the heel and takes the pressure off the tendon.

Cartilage

A high percentage of players, particularly professionals, need cartilages removed from their knees at some stage of their careers. Modern key-hole type of surgery makes this less of an ordeal than in the past but it is still advisable to delay a return to full training until medical clearance has been obtained. Too many players try to play too soon after an cartilage operation and often need further surgery. 'Don't come back before you are ready,' must be the advice to any player who has had a knee operation. But it is essential to build up the thigh muscles gradually with regular exercising.

Concussion

Few players can expect to go through their careers without being concussed at some stage, especially if they are centre-halves or strikers. The injured player should be examined, and if there is any doubt about his condition after submitting him to a simple eye test – asking him to look at a moving finger on the line of his nose – he should not be allowed to continue playing. As a safeguard he should be taken to hospital.

One of the hazards of being temporarily knocked out is that the player might swallow his tongue, which can prove fatal. Referees now have to take a simple medical test which includes the correct treatment of a player who has swallowed his tongue. It is advisable that the club's trainer also has the same knowledge.

Dislocation

Goalkeepers frequently stub a little finger into the ground and dislocate it, and usually the trainer can put it back straight away. But with bigger fingers and thumbs, it may be necessary to take the patient to a doctor or a hospital.

Back Pain

Half the population suffer from back trouble at some stage of their lives and footballers are no exception. Rest is the only cure and I recommend those with back problems to sleep on a hard bed, or put a board under their mattress, and wear soft-heeled shoes with artificial soles.

Neck Injuries

Players who are always twisting their necks to head the ball suffer problems with their neck. Stretching exercises before matches can help. In extreme cases doctors will urge the use of a surgical collar.

Broken ribs

Cracking a rib is a painful business and there is no cure except rest. It can take up to six weeks before the player is ready to play again, depending on how many ribs have been cracked.

Muscle Strains

These are to the thigh, hamstring or calf and vary in the degree of damage to the muscle. Most injuries of this type require stretching movement to stimulate recovery, otherwise the player will be out of action longer. The advice of a physiotherapist should be sought.

Sprained ankle

There is hardly a footballer playing who has not sprained an ankle. Even with a mild sprain, it is advisable for the player to come off the field and have ice applied to help reduce the inevitable swelling. Later, he will find that immersion into hot then cold water, alternately, will speed recovery.

A strapping will be needed, preferably a crêpe bandage wrapped around the joint in a figure-of-eight pattern. With more serious sprains, there can be damage to the ligaments and a longer period of rest is required.

Many players strap their ankles before taking part in a match. Trevor Brooking always used to. But modern experts do not recommend the practice. They believe a weak ankle can be strengthened if weight is put on it and it is not molly-coddled. Stretching exercises undertaken regularly are said to be of more benefit than a protective strapping.

In the case of severe ligament damage, the joint sometimes has to be encased in Plaster of Paris to make sure it has complete rest.

Twisted Knee

The knee is the most complex joint in the human body and is the one which is most commonly injured in all sports. The stress of the modern game puts enormous strains on the knee and it is not surprising that it often succumbs.

Swelling is the first sign that something is amiss, and then a consultation with a doctor is a priority. He can determine the extent of the injury and the treatment. In most cases the application of ice and hot and cold compresses can reduce the swelling. Heat is a healer and ultra-sonic treatment, where it is available, is most helpful to knee, ankle and associated injuries.

Phantom Injuries or Play-Acting

These are very prevalent! It is easy to detect when a player is shamming. He will roll over or make some obvious demonstration. The West Germans, who are possibly the worst offenders, will roll over and over. If a player is really injured, he will stay still because it is painful to move!

Those who feign injuries are cheating the referee, the opposing team and the crowd. I fully endorse the action of any referee who cautions offenders for ungentlemanly conduct of this nature. Fortunately, feigning injury is not as common in Britain as it is on the Continent and in South American football.

Conditioning Training

It is important to realise that when players start to mature, they need more conditioning work. They need to build up stamina and try to become faster with this in mind.

On the following pages you will find a plan of aerobic and anaerobic working exercises suitable for fourteen-year-olds and upwards. During pre-season training you should pick out an example from each section and include them in each training session along with the ball work. I suggest you do the physical work at the end of your training session. Some coaches just do one conditioning session on fitness alone.

The plan of conditioning work is divided into two sections – Long Distance (Aerobic) Stamina Work and Sprinting (Anaerobic) Shuttle Runs. In each section there are six alternative exercises:

Section I – Stamina Work

1 Twelve-Minute Run
2 Cross-Country
3 Interval Running
4 Box to Box
5 Increase Demand
6 Football Running

Section II – Shuttle Runs

1 5-, 10-, 15-, 20-, 25-metre Runs
2 Doggies (30 metres)
3 10 metres x 10 metres – Check Boards
4 Shoot at Goal
5 In and Out of the Flags
6 30-,40-,50-, 60-metre Sprints

A full description of each exercise follows.

I Stamina Work

1 *Twelve-Minute Run (Cooper Test)*
The players run around a plotted course for twelve minutes. After twelve minutes, the distance for each individual player is measured. The next time he repeats the exercise he must try and beat his distance to show improvement.

2 *Cross-Country*
The run should be approximately four miles. Look for a route with hills and trees. The run should be timed for each individual player. Each time he runs he must try to beat his best time.

3 *Interval Running*
This is ideal if you have a running track available. The run should not be more than 200 metres. The players run together. They run the distance six times with a rest between each run. The rest should be similar to the time it takes to do the run. Overload by using one of two methods – either shorten the rest between each run or do more runs, eight for example.

4 *Box to Box*
This is another form of interval training, except that it is very applicable to footballers. The players line up in pairs on the edge of the penalty-box. When the whistle goes, the first player in each pair runs back. When he arrives back he touches his partner off. He now rests. His partner does exactly the same run. They keep going until they have both completed six runs each. This must be timed. You can overload by introducing

cones or hurdles in the run, so that players have to jump or zigzag.

5 Increase Demand

The players run in groups. From the starting position they sprint to the first flag, then slowly jog around the pitch back to the starting position. Next time they sprint to the second flag, then jog to the starting position. Finally they sprint to the third flag, then jog to the starting position. They keep going until they have reached the sixth flag.

6 Football Running

This is controlled by the coach. When he shouts, the players either sprint, jog or walk. The players do two laps – rest – two laps – rest – two laps – finish. The rest should be walking for one minute.

II Shuttle Runs

1 5-,10-,15-,20-,25-metre Runs

The player runs from the start-line out to each cone and back in turn. He rests for one minute, then goes again. The player should try and do three in his first session. But when he is in shape, ten should be completed. The run-times must be improved.

2 Doggies (30 metres)

The player does three runs with ten seconds' rest between each run. One run is out to the 30-metre cone and back.

3 10 metres x 10 metres – Check Boards (Fig. 116)

Using check boards so that players can turn quickly. The player goes there and back five times, completing 100 metres. He then rests for twenty seconds before he does it again. At the first session the player should do at least three, aiming for twelve when he is fit.

START   *Fig. 116*

10m

4 Shoot at Goal (Fig. 117)

Three balls are put on the edge of the penalty-box. From the half-way line the player runs and shoots the first ball, trying to score. He then turns, goes back to the starting position and runs in again to shoot. He then turns, runs back to the start and goes again to shoot the final ball. He can build this up by having more balls or taking a rest before he goes again.

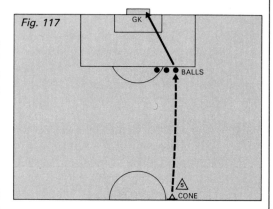

Fig. 117 GK BALLS CONE

5 In and Out of Flags

The flags are angled 10 metres apart. The first player goes in and out of the flags to the furthest one, turns and runs straight back to the start. After twenty seconds' rest he goes again. At first, three runs is enough, but fit players should aim for ten.

6 30-,40-,50-,60-metre Sprints

Working in groups of three players, the first player runs out to the 30-metre marker and back, then the second man goes and after him the third man. The first man then runs out to the 40-metre marker and back. In turn, the other two players run. The exercise must be kept going until they have completed the 60-metre run. This work is looking for good technique sprinting, good leg and arm action.

Weight Training

If a player wants to be faster and more powerful, if he wants to withstand and cope with the physical aspects of the game, there is only one answer – weight training.

Weight training is still treated with scepticism in football, mainly through ignorance and prejudice. There are those who say, 'It makes you muscle-bound' or 'It puts on too much weight,' but in athletics weight training is one of the most important facets of training programmes.

I do not see Steve Cram or Seb Coe muscle-bound or putting on too much weight. Athletes like Allan Wells and Daley Thompson use weights to make their thighs more powerful and the top half of their body stronger and better defined. It makes them run faster. They still have to do plenty of sprint training but, after obtaining a good technique, the bulk of their training work will be to strengthen their legs.

The long-jumpers, high-jumpers and triple-jump men only get longer, higher and better through increasing the power of the legs. And that comes from weight training. I do not see any of them overweight or loaded down with muscle. Quite the opposite, they are terrific examples of athleticism and agility which have come from proper training.

Equipment

If you have access to any of the modern weight-training machines, that is a bonus. They are easy to use, the exercises are set out and they are safe. It is easy to check the amount of weight you are working with, which is vitally important in weight training.

But you do not need all that sophisticated equipment. All you really need is bars, six feet or two metres in length, small bars for dumb-bell work and a variety of weight discs, ranging from 5 lbs or 2½ kilos up to 25 lbs or 10 kilos, totalling approximately 400 lbs or 200 kilos. Bar clips are needed to ensure the discs stay on the bar while you are working.

Technique

Technique is all-important. Without it, there is a real risk of sustaining serious back injury. The coach in charge must know how to teach the lifting technique. He should also be very diligent during training sessions, making sure players do not stray from the proper technique and safety rules of weight work.

The technique of lifting the bar (*Fig. 118*)
Eyes should be looking up, focusing on something just above the head.

The back should be straight from the neck to the backside, chest pressed forwards a little.

Fig. 118

Arms should be straight, hands feeling for the bar outside the knees.

Thighs should be parallel to the ground.

Feet should be shoulder-width apart, toes just poking under the bar.

The lift should start by straightening the legs. When the bar leaves the floor, the arms continue the pull, lifting the bar to the position needed.

At the end of the exercise, putting the weight down is just as important. The head should stay up, eyes focused high. Bend the legs, push the chest forwards keeping the back straight. Lower the weight gently, release the hands once the weight is grounded.

Having developed a sound technique, the work can be started. As players in general have poor upper body and arm strength, it is advisable to select two upper body exercises and one for the legs. The following pages contain illustrations and full descriptions of all exercises. The first session could comprise these three exercises:

First Exercise	This means you do eight of each exercise three times and rest between each eight. It is ideal if you work in threes and take turns to do the exercise, i.e., No. 1 does eight and rests while No. 2 does eight, then No. 3 does eight. Then No. 1 does his second eight and so on. This ensures the proper rest between exercises. Use this routine on all weight work.
Curls 3 x 8	
Second Exercise	
Half-Squat 3 x 8	
Third Exercise	
Bench Press 3 x 8	

Leg work – one exercise – half-squat.

Upper body – two exercises – curls, bench presses.

Start with a good twenty-minute warm-up, plenty of jogging and stretching exercises.

What weight to have on the bar

I suggest half your body weight, i.e., if you weigh 150 lbs, start with 75 lbs on the bars. You can then adjust accordingly. If you struggle, take some weight off. If you are doing the exercise easily, put more weight on.

It is vital you keep a check on the weight you are using. Make yourself a chart giving date, exercise, weight used.

When to put more weight on the bar

If you are doing the third eight of the exercise easily, put another 5 lbs on each end of the bar. You should always find the third one of each exercise hard-going. That is when you are building the power.

After four months, change your exercises to lift and press, step-ups and alternative arm curls. Not only will the change of exercises make the work more interesting, but it will attack different muscles.

After a few more months, when the body is getting stronger, build up the weight and cut down on the repetitions, e.g.

Half-squat 3 x 4 x 300 lbs (increased from 100 lbs).

How often should you do weight training?

During the summer – three sessions a week. During the season with one game a week – two sessions, between Monday and Wednesday. During the season with two games a week – one session on Monday morning.

As with all training items, the occasional rest helps the body and rekindles the enthusiasm. After three months' work, have a month's rest.

Half-Squat (Legs)
(*Fig. 119*)
With the bar across the shoulders, bend the legs until the thighs and backside are parallel with the ground. Then push hard to straighten the legs. If the feet leave the ground, that is fine.

Do not let your backside down too low. As a safety precaution put a chair behind you so that you cannot go lower than the seat.

Lift and Press (Legs and upper body) (*Fig. 120*)
From the ground you lift the bar in one lift to the chest, pause and then press to straight arms above the head, and then back to the ground.

Fig. 119

Fig. 120

Curls (Upper body) (*Fig. 121*)
Holding the bar, palms facing away from you, arms straight and shoulder-width apart down by the thighs. From the thighs lift the weight with the palms and arms outwards up to your chest, and then slowly lower down again.

Bench Press (Upper body) (*Fig. 122*)
Lying on the bench, arms straight and reaching for the sky, you need a partner to place the weight in your hands. Once in position, bend the arms so that the bar virtually touches the chest and then press the bar to straight-arm position again.

Fig. 121

Fig. 122

Fig. 123

Fig. 124

Step-ups (Legs) (*Fig. 123*)
Pick the weight up and
place it on your shoulders.
Face the bench and place
the left foot on the bench.
Step up with the right leg
following. Straighten the
legs on the bench, then step
off with the right leg first.

Press behind Neck (Upper
body) (*Fig. 124*)
Pick the bar up and place it
behind the neck. Straighten
the arms above the head,
hold, then bend the arms
and replace the bar behind
the head on to the neck and
shoulders in the starting
position.

Alternate Arm Curl using Dumb-bells (Upper body) (*Fig. 125*)
Hold the dumb-bells, arms straight down by the thighs and palms facing outwards. Alternately lift arms (as in the curl) up to the chest and slowly back down again.

Alternate Arm Press above Head using Dumb-bells (Upper body) (*Fig. 126*)
Start with arms straight down by the thighs. Alternately lift arms above the head and slowly back down again.

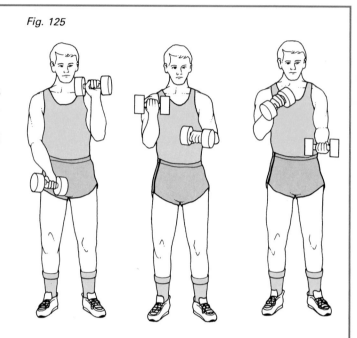

Fig. 125

Fig. 126

Fig. 127

Fig. 128

Both Arms Lift using Dumb-bells (Upper body) (*Fig. 127*)
Start with arms down by the sides of the body. Lift both arms together out wide into the horizontal position, slowly lower.

Alternate Arm Lift and Turn from Bent Position using one Dumb-bell (Upper body) (*Fig. 128*)
Bend forward, legs flexed, feet shoulder-width apart, arms straight. With one hand grab the dumb-bell, lift and turn at the waist with this arm above the head. Slowly lower, then use the opposite arm and hand.

Fitness at the Junior Level

Youngsters play football because they enjoy it, or should do. Until the age of sixteen it is not necessary for them to train. Their bodies are still growing and their enthusiasm is such that fitness comes naturally to them.

As they get older, the demands of the game change. A prepared team will beat a side that is not prepared, if all other things are equal.

From the Ages of Eleven to Fourteen

I would not recommend boys up to fourteen to do any kind of training. The game itself will keep them fit. What they should be trying to do at this age is to improve their 'feel' of the ball. They should be encouraged to work individually with the ball.

Wiel Coerver, the Dutch coach, says boys should be aiming to have 6,000 touches a day. That is rather a lot! Around 1,000 touches would be more realistic. Kicking the ball against a wall is ideal practice and does not need a lot of space.

Many of the great players of the past have used a wall to improve their skills. Bobby Charlton, for example, used to take a tennis ball to school with him and use it to kick against houses and walls on his way home. More sustained practice can be undertaken against a garage or side of a house. The earlier the boy starts using both feet in these exercises, the more likely it is he will develop into a two-footed player.

There are three areas in which boys of eleven to fourteen should be urged to concentrate their efforts:

1 Juggling the ball, keeping it up with feet, head, shoulders, knees etc., so that they get used to the ball and master it. Ball-juggling of the type made famous by former West Bromwich Albion player David Burnside, now a coach, was decried at the time as an irrelevance and unrelated to what football should be all about. But like most modern coaches, I dispute that. The first priority of a young footballer is to be able to control and work with the ball. If his touch and feel for it are good from an early age, he has a better chance of developing into a good player.

2 Running with the ball. This is another simple exercise which, if necessary, can be done alone, dribbling around obstacles. But if other boys are present, the boy on the ball can learn to take them on and dribble around them, copying the tricks he has been shown or has seen on television.

3 The playing of small-sided games. I do not recommend boys up to fourteen taking part in too many matches over the full size of the pitch. The most they should be asked to do is to take part in a game over half the pitch.

The West Germans pioneered an idea of marking 'grids' for boys to work in about twenty years ago, and it is a system I recommend. These 'grids', or small areas, can be as small as ten metres square, with one boy trying to take the ball off three others who pass it between them (*Fig. 129*)

The purpose is to practise passing techniques and good running off the ball. The size of the 'grids' is optional. They can be increased to fifteen square metres, twenty square metres and so on, with the number of

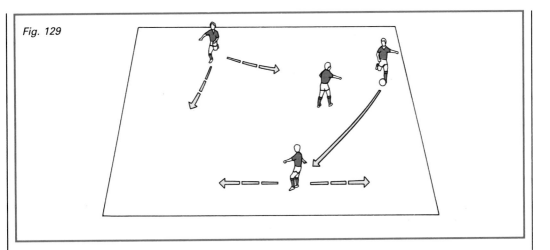

Fig. 129

boys taking part increasing correspondingly. The boys are swapped around, all taking turns to be the 'piggy in the middle'.

After the age of twelve, boys will be wanting to play matches but the emphasis should still be on small-sided games and teaching the skills. Small-sided matches, six v. six, over half the pitch are a sensible compromise.

When it is eleven v. eleven over the whole pitch, the physical side comes into it so much more and the bigger, stronger boys will monopolise the ball. This is why small-sided practices are so important, to give the small boy the same opportunity as the big boy.

By the time boys are ready to play matches, they should be shown the importance of maintaining their position and not running all over the field after the ball. I recommend that junior teams use a four-three-three system which is balanced. It is easier to use than other systems and boys can start learning their positional responsibilities.

The danger is playing too many matches. Many of our best young players are expected to take part in four or five matches a week, which is far too many. It increases the risk of injury and can dull the enthusiasm of even

the keenest youngster. Two matches a week are ample. At this age much more time should be spent practising skills than playing in matches.

The coach must accept that there is a risk that youngsters will lose interest if they have to do what *he* wants them to do all the time. He must acknowledge that there will be a time when he lets them have their own way, and that will mean letting them have an eleven v. eleven game, preferably on a smaller-sized pitch, at the end of sessions.

Boys like copying their heroes and that means eleven v. eleven, not small-sided games. A 'proper' game at the end of the session is a good way to wind up and it helps them learn their positional responsibilities.

From the Ages of Fourteen to Sixteen

Skill and ball work should still command the attention of the boys. But their bodies are strong enough for them to begin circuit training and shuttle runs, which build up the strength of the legs and help mobility.

Boys of this age will have a greater sense of responsibility about positional play and their role in the team. They will know when to go forward and when to stay back. A more competitive edge will be coming into their game.

From the Ages of Sixteen to Eighteen

Suddenly, it is no longer a game played purely for fun. Boys wanting to make football their career will be keen to join a club. Instead of being a game, it becomes a career. Attitudes have to harden, otherwise the boy will become one of the many drop-outs in the professional game.

There will be demands for success. The result of each game becomes important, and boys have to get used to finding their performances being analysed in a critical fashion. They have to work on stamina training, using weights and doing much more physical work. They have to be fitter and stronger and learn the tactical side of the game. Especially at the lower levels, it is important that boys should be coached in an encouraging, positive manner. Too many junior games are ruined by the continual, carping criticism of team managers and relatives. Though a harder element of competition is introduced, it is still a game to be enjoyed.

APPENDICES
AND
INDEX

Appendix I: Laws of the Game

The Laws of the Game and Decisions of the International Board that follow are reproduced with the special permission of FIFA, and the text is the official text as published by FIFA.

LAW I

The Field of Play

The Field of Play and appurtenances shall be as shown in the following plan:

(1) Dimensions: the field of play shall be rectangular, its length being not more than 130 yards nor less than 100 yards and its breadth not more than 100 yards nor less than 50 yards. (In International Matches the length shall be not more than 120 yards nor less than 110 yards and the breadth not more than 80 yards nor less than 70 yards.) The length shall in all cases exceed the breadth.

(2) Marking: The field of play shall be marked with distinctive lines, not more than 5 inches in width, not by a V-shaped rut, in accordance with the plan, the longer boundary lines being called the touch-lines and the shorter the goal-lines. A flag on a post not less than 5 feet high and having a non-pointed top, shall be placed at each corner; a similar flag-post may be placed opposite the half-way line on each side of the field of play, not less than 1 yard outside the touch-line. A half-way line of play shall be indicated by a suitable mark and a circle with a 10-yard radius shall be marked round it.

(3) The Goal-Area: At each end of the field of play two lines shall be drawn at right angles to the goal-line, 6 yards from each goal-post. These shall extend into the field of play for a distance of 6 yards and shall be joined by a line drawn parallel with the goal-line. Each of the spaces enclosed by these lines and the goal-line shall be called a goal-area.

(4) The Penalty-Area: At each end of the field of play two lines shall be drawn at right angles to the goal-lines, 18 yards from each goal-post. These shall extend into the field of play for a distance of 18 yards and shall be joined by a line drawn parallel with the goal-line. Each of the spaces enclosed by these lines and the goal-line shall be called a penalty-area. A suitable mark shall be made within each penalty-area, 12 yards from the mid-point of the goal-line, measured along an undrawn line at right angles thereto. These shall be the penalty-kick marks. From each penalty-kick mark an arc of a circle, having a radius of 10 yards, shall be drawn outside the penalty-area.

(5) The Corner-Area: From each corner flag-post a quarter circle, having a radius of 1 yard, shall be drawn inside the field of play.

(6) The Goals: The goals shall be placed on the centre of each goal-line and shall consist of two upright posts, equidistant from the corner-flags and 8 yards apart (inside measurement), joined by a horizontal crossbar the lower edge of which shall be 8 feet from the ground. The width and depth of the goal-posts and the width and depth of the crossbars shall not exceed 5 inches. The goal-posts and the crossbars shall have the same width.

Nets† may be attached to the posts, crossbars and ground behind the goals. They should be appropriately supported and be so placed as to allow the goalkeeper ample room.

⅜ inch	. . . 0.010 metre
14 ounces	. . . 396 grams
16 ounces	. . . 453 grams
8.5 lb/sq in	. . . 600 gr/cm²
15.6 lb/sq in	. . . 1,100 gr/cm²

Decisions of the International Board

(1) In International Matches the dimensions of the field of play shall be: maximum 110 x 75 metres; minimum 100 x 64 metres.

(2) National Associations must adhere strictly to these dimensions. Each National Association organising an International Match must advise the visiting Association, before the match, of the place and the dimensions of the field of play.

(3) The board has approved this conversion table of measurements for the Laws of the Game:

130 yards	. . . 120 metres
120 yards	. . . 110 metres
110 yards	. . . 100 metres
100 yards	. . . 90 metres
80 yards	. . . 75 metres
70 yards	. . . 64 metres
50 yards	. . . 45 metres
18 yards	. . . 16.5 metres
12 yards	. . . 11 metres
10 yards	. . . 9.15 metres
8 yards	. . . 7.32 metres
6 yards	. . . 5.50 metres
1 yard	. . . 1 metre
8 feet	. . . 2.44 metres
5 feet	. . . 1.50 metres
28 inches	. . . 0.71 metre
27 inches	. . . 0.68 metre
9 inches	. . . 0.22 metre
5 inches	. . . 0.12 metre
¾ inch	. . . 0.019 metre
½ inch	. . . 0.0127 metre

† *Goal nets.* The use of nets made of hemp, jute or nylon is permitted. The nylon strings may, however, not be thinner than those made of hemp or jute.

(4) The goal-line shall be marked the same width as the depth of the goal-posts and the crossbar, so that the goal-line and goal-post will conform to the same interior and exterior edges.

(5) The 6 yards (for the outline of the goal-area) and 18 yards (for the outline of the penalty-area) which have to be measured along the goal-line, must start from the inner sides of the goal-posts.

(6) The space within the inside areas of the field of play includes the width of the lines marking these areas.

(7) All Associations shall provide standard equipment, particularly in International Matches when the Laws of the Game must be complied with in every respect and especially with regard to the size of the ball and other equipment which must conform to the regulations. All cases of failure to provide standard equipment must be reported to FIFA.

(8) In a match played under the rules of a competition, if the crossbar becomes displaced or broken, play shall be stopped and the match abandoned unless the crossbar has been repaired and replaced in position or a new one provided without such being a danger to the players. A rope is not considered to be a satisfactory substitute for a crossbar.

In a Friendly match, by mutual consent, play may be resumed without the crossbar, provided it has been removed and no longer constitutes a danger to the players. In these circumstances, a rope may be used as a substitute for a crossbar. If a rope is not used and the ball crosses the goal-line at a point which in the opinion of the Referee is below where the crossbar should have been, he shall award a goal.

The game shall be restarted by the Referee dropping the ball at the place where it was when play was stopped, unless it was within the goal-area at that time, in which case it shall be dropped on that part of the goal-area line which runs parallel to the goal-line, at the point nearest to where the ball was when play was stopped.

(9) National Associations may specify such maximum and minimum dimensions for the crossbars and goal-posts, within the limits laid down in Law I, as they consider appropriate.

10) Goal-posts and crossbars must be made of wood, metal or other approved material as decided from time to time by the International FA Board. They may be square, rectangular, round, half-round or elliptical in shape. Goal-posts and crossbars made of other materials and in other shapes are not permitted.

(11) 'Curtain-raisers' to International Matches should only be played following agreement on the day of the match, and taking into account the condition of the field of play, between representatives of the two Associations and the Referee (of the International Match).

(12) National Associations, particularly in International Matches, should
- restrict the number of photographers around the field of play,
- have a line ('photographers' line') marked behind the goal-lines at least 2 metres from the corner-flag going through a point situated at least 3.5 metres behind the intersection of the goal-line with the line marking the goal-area to a point situated at least six metres behind the goal-posts,
- prohibit photographers from passing over these lines,
- forbid the use of artificial lighting in the form of 'flashlights'.

LAW II
The Ball

The ball shall be spherical; the outer casing shall be of leather or other approved materials. No material shall be used in its construction which might prove dangerous to the players.

The circumference of the ball shall not be more than 28 inches and not less than 27 inches. The weight of the ball at the start of the game shall not be more than 16 ounces not less than 14 ounces. The pressure shall be equal to 0.6–1.1 atmosphere, (= 600–1100gr/cm^2) at sea level. The ball shall not be changed during the game unless authorised by the Referee.

Decisions of the International Board

(1) The ball used in any match shall be considered the property of the Association or Club on whose ground the match is played, and at the close of play it must be returned to the Referee.

(2) The International Board, from time to time, shall decide what constitutes approved materials. Any approved material shall be certified as such by the International Board.

(3) The Board has approved these equivalents of the weights specified in the Law: 14 to 16 ounces = 396 to 453 grammes.

(4) If the ball bursts or becomes deflated during the course of a match, the game shall

be stopped and restarted by dropping the new ball at the place where the first ball became defective, unless it was within the goal-area at that time, in which case it shall be dropped on that part of the goal-area line which runs parallel to the goal-line, at the point nearest to where the ball was when play was stopped.

(5) If this happens during a stoppage of the game (place-kick, goal-kick, corner-kick, free-kick, penalty-kick or throw-in) the game shall be restarted accordingly.

LAW III
Number of Players

(1) A match shall be played by two teams, each consisting of not more than eleven players, one of whom shall be the goalkeeper.

(2) Substitutes may be used in any match played under the rules of an official competition at FIFA, Confederation or National Association level, subject to the following conditions:

a) that the authority of the International Association(s) or National Association(s) concerned has been obtained;

b) that, subject to the restriction contained in the following paragraph (c), the rules of a competition shall state how many, if any, substitutes may be used, and

c) that a team shall not be permitted to use more than two substitutes in any match, who must be chosen from not more than five players whose names shall be given to the Referee prior to the commencement of the match.

(3) Substitutes may be used in any other match, provided that the two teams concerned reach agreement on a maximum number, not exceeding five, and that the

terms of such agreement are intimated to the Referee, before the match. If the Referee is not informed, or if the teams fail to reach agreement, no more than two substitutes shall be permitted. In all cases the substitutes must be chosen from not more than five players whose names shall be given to the Referee prior to the commencement of the match.

(4) Any of the other players may change places with the goalkeeper, provided that the Referee is informed before the change is made, and provided also, that the change is made during a stoppage in the game.

(5) When a goalkeeper or any other player is to be replaced by a substitute, the following conditions shall be observed:

a) The Referee shall be informed of the proposed substitution, before it is made.

b) The substitute shall not enter the field of play until the player he is replacing has left, and then only after having received a signal from the Referee.

c) He shall enter the field during a stoppage in the game, and at the half-way line.

d) A player who has been replaced shall not take any further part in the game.

e) A substitute shall be subject to the authority and jurisdiction of the Referee whether called upon to play or not.

f) The substitution is completed when the substitute enters the field of play, from which moment he becomes a player and the player whom he is replacing ceases to be a player.

Punishment

a) Play shall not be stopped for an infringement of paragraph 4. The players concerned shall be cautioned immediately the ball goes out of play.

b) If a substitute enters the field of play without the authority of the Referee, play shall be stopped. The substitute shall be cautioned or sent off according to the circumstances. The game shall be restarted by the Referee dropping the ball at the place where it was when play was stopped, unless it was within the goal-area at that time, in which case it shall be dropped on that part of the goal-area line which runs parallel to the goal-line, at the point nearest to where the ball was when play was stopped.

c) For any other infringement of this Law, the player concerned shall be cautioned, and if the game is stopped by the Referee, to administer the caution, it shall be re-started by an indirect free-kick, to be taken by a player of the opposing team from the place where the ball was, when play was stopped, subject to the over-riding conditions imposed in Law XIII.

Decisions of the International Board

(1) The minimum number of players in a team is left to the discretion of National Associations.

(2) The Board is of the opinion that a match should not be considered valid if there are fewer than seven players in either of the teams.

3) A player who has been ordered off before play begins may be replaced only by one of the named substitutes. The kick-off must not be delayed to allow the substitute to join his team.

A player who has been ordered off after play has started may not be replaced.

A named substitute who has been ordered off, either before or after play has started, may not be replaced. (This decision relates only to players who are ordered off under Law XII. It does not apply to players who have infringed Law IV.)

LAW IV
Players' Equipment

A player shall not wear anything which is dangerous to another player. Footwear (boots or shoes) must conform to the following standard:

a) Bars shall be made of leather or rubber and shall be transverse and flat, not less than half an inch in width and shall extend the total width of the sole and be rounded at the corners.

b) Studs which are independently mounted on the sole and are replaceable shall be made of leather, rubber, aluminium, plastic or similar material and shall be solid. With the exception of that part of the stud forming the base, which shall not protrude from the sole more than one quarter of an inch, studs shall be round in plan and not less than half an inch in diameter. Where studs are tapered, the minimum diameter of any section of the study must not be less than half an inch. Where metal seating for the screw type is used, this seating must be embedded in the sole of the footwear and any attachment screw shall be part of the stud. Other than the metal seating for the screw type of stud, no metal plates even though covered with leather or rubber shall be worn, neither studs which are threaded to allow them to be screwed on to a base screw that is fixed by nails or otherwise to the soles of footwear, nor studs which, apart from the base, have any form of protruding edge rim or relief marking or ornament should be allowed.

c) Studs which are moulded as an integral

part of the sole and are not replaceable shall be made of rubber, plastic polyurethene or similar soft materials. Provided that there are no fewer than ten studs on the sole, they shall have a minimum diameter of three-eighths of an inch (10mm). Additional supporting material to stabilise studs of soft materials, and ridges which shall not protrude more than 5mm from the sole and moulded to strengthen it, shall be permitted provided that they are in no way dangerous to other players. In all other respects they shall conform to the general requirements of this Law.

d) Combined bars and studs may be worn, provided the whole conforms to the general requirements of this Law. Neither bars nor studs on the soles or heels shall project more than three-quarters of an inch. If nails are used they shall be driven in flush with the surface.

The goalkeeper shall wear colours which distinguish him from the other players and from the Referee.

Punishment

For any infringement of this Law, the player at fault shall be sent off the field of play to adjust his equipment and he shall not return without first reporting to the Referee, who shall satisfy himself that the player's equipment is in order; the player shall only re-enter the game at a moment when the ball has ceased to be in play.

Decisions of the International Board

(1) The usual equipment of a player is a jersey or shirt, shorts, stockings, and footwear. In a match played under the rules of a competition, players need not wear boots or shoes, but shall wear jersey or shirt, shorts, or track suit or similar trousers, and stockings.

(2) The Law does not insist that boots or shoes must be worn. However, in competition matches Referees should not allow one or a few players to play without footwear when all the other players are so equipped.

(3) In International Matches, International Competitions, International Club Competitions and Friendly Matches between clubs of different National Associations, the Referee, prior to the start of the game, shall inspect the players' footwear, and prevent any player whose footwear does not conform to the requirements of this Law from playing until such time as it does comply.

The rules of any competition may include a similar provision.

(4) If the Referee finds that a player is wearing articles not permitted by the Laws and which may constitute a danger to other players, he shall order him to take them off. If he fails to carry out the Referee's instruction, the player shall not take part in the match.

(5) A player who has been prevented from taking part in the game or a player who has been sent off the field for infringing Law IV must report to the Referee during a stoppage of the game and may not enter or re-enter the field of play unless and until the Referee has satisfied himself that the player is no longer infringing Law IV.

(6) A player who has been prevented from taking part in a game or who has been sent off because of an infringement of Law IV, and who enters or re-enters the field of play to join or rejoin his team, in breach of the conditions of the Law XII, shall be cautioned. If the Referee stops the game to administer the caution, the game shall be restarted by an indirect free-kick, taken by a player of the opposing side, from the place

where the ball was when the Referee stopped the game, subject to the over-riding conditions imposed in Law XIII.

LAW V
Referees

A Referee shall be appointed to officiate in each game. His authority and the exercise of the powers granted to him by the Laws of the Game commence as soon as he enters the field of play.

His power of penalising shall extend to offences committed when play has been temporarily suspended, or when the ball is out of play. His decision on points of fact connected with the play shall be final, so far as the result of the game is concerned. He shall:

a) Enforce the Laws.

b) Refrain from penalising in cases where he is satisfied that, by doing so, he would be giving an advantage to the offending team.

c) Keep a record of the game, act as timekeeper and allow the full or agreed time, adding thereto all time lost through accident or other cause.

d) Have discretionary power to stop the game for any infringement of the Laws and to suspend or terminate the game whenever, by reason of the elements, interference by spectators, or other cause, he deems such stoppage necessary. In such a case he shall submit a detailed report to the competent authority, within the stipulated time, and in accordance with the provisions set up by the National Association under whose jurisdiction the match was played. Reports will be deemed to be made when received in the ordinary course of post.

e) From the time he enters the field of play, caution any player guilty of misconduct or ungentlemanly behaviour and, if he persists, suspend him from further participation in the game. In such cases the Referee shall send the name of the offender to the competent authority, within the stipulated time, and in accordance with the provisions set up by the National Association under whose jurisdiction the match was played. Reports will be deemed to be made when received in the ordinary course of post.

f) Allow no person other than the players and Linesmen to enter the field of play without his permission.

g) Stop the game if, in his opinion, a player has been seriously injured; have the player removed as soon as possible from the field of play, and immediately resume the game. If a player is slightly injured, the game shall not be stopped until the ball has ceased to be in play. A player who is able to go to the touch- or goal-line for attention of any kind, shall not be treated on the field of play.

h) Send off the field of play, any player who, in his opinion, is guilty of violent conduct, serious foul play, or the use of foul or abusive language.

i) Signal for recommencement of the game after all stoppages.

j) Decide that the ball provided for a match meets with the requirements of Law II.

Decisions of the International Board

(1) Referees in International Matches shall wear a blazer or blouse the colour of which is distinct from the colours worn by the contesting teams.

(2) Referees for International Matches will

be selected from a neutral country unless the countries concerned agree to appoint their own officials.

(3) The Referee must be chosen from the official list of International Referees. This need not apply to Amateur and Youth International matches.

(4) The Referee shall report to the appropriate authority misconduct or any misdemeanour on the part of spectators, officials, players, named substitutes or other persons which take place either on the field of play or in its vicinity at any time prior to, during, or after the match in question so that appropriate action can be taken by the authority concerned.

(5) Linesmen are assistants of the Referee. In no case shall the Referee consider the intervention of a Linesman if he himself has seen the incident and from his position on the field, is better able to judge. With this reserve, and the Linesman neutral, the Referee can consider the intervention and if the information of the Linesman applies to that phase of the game immediately before the scoring of a goal, the Referee may act thereon and cancel the goal.

(6) The Referee, however, can only reverse his first decision so long as the game has not been restarted.

(7) If the Referee has decided to apply the advantage clause and to let the game proceed, he cannot revoke his decision if the presumed advantage has not been realised, even though he has not, by any gesture, indicated his decision. This does not exempt the offending player from being dealt with by the Referee.

(8) The Laws of the Game are intended to provide that games should be played with as little interference as possible, and in this view it is the duty of Referees to penalise only deliberate breaches of the Law. Constant whistling for trifling and doubtful breaches produces bad feeling and loss of temper on the part of the players and spoils the pleasure of spectators.

(9) By paragraph (d) of Law V the Referee is empowered to terminate a match in the event of grave disorder, but he has no power or right to decide, in such event, that either team is disqualified and thereby the loser of the match. He must send a detailed report to the proper authority who alone has power to deal further with this matter.

(10) If a player commits two infringements of a different nature at the same time, the Referee shall punish the more serious offence.

(11) It is the duty of the Referee to act upon the information of neutral Linesmen with regard to incidents that do not come under the personal notice of the Referee.

(12) The Referee shall not allow any person to enter the field until play has stopped, and only then, if he has given him a signal to do so, nor shall he allow coaching from the boundary lines.

LAW VI

Linesmen

Two Linesmen shall be appointed, whose duty (subject to the decision of the Referee) shall be to indicate when the ball is out of play, which side is entitled to the corner-kick, goal-kick or throw-in, and when a substitution is desired. They shall also assist the Referee to control the game in accordance with the Laws. In the event of undue interference or improper conduct by a Linesman, the Referee shall dispense with his services and arrange for a substitute to be appointed. (The matter shall be reported by the Referee to the competent authority.) The Linesmen should be equipped with flags by the Club on whose ground the match is played.

Decisions of the International Board

(1) Linesmen, when neutral, shall draw the Referee's attention to any breach of the Laws of the Game of which they become aware if they consider that the Referee may not have seen it, but the Referee shall always be the judge of the decision to be taken.

(2) National Associations are advised to appoint official Referees of neutral nationality to act as Linesmen in International Matches.

(3) In International Matches, Linesmen's flags shall be of a vivid colour, bright reds and yellows. Such flags are recommended for use in all other matches.

(4) A Linesman may be subject to disciplinary action only upon a report of the Referee for unjustified interference or insufficient assistance.

LAW VII
Duration of the Game

The duration of the game shall be two equal periods of 45 minutes, unless otherwise mutually agreed upon, subject to the following:
(a) Allowance shall be made in either period for all time lost through substitution, the transport from the field of injured players, time-wasting or other cause, the amount of which shall be a matter for the discretion of the Referee.

(b) Time shall be extended to permit a penalty-kick being taken at or after the expiration of the normal period in either half.

At half-time the interval shall not exceed five minutes except by consent of the Referee.

Decisions of the International Board

(1) If a match has been stopped by the Referee before the completion of the time specified in the rules, for any reason stated in Law V, it must be replayed in full unless the rules of the competition concerned provide for the result of the match at the time of such stoppage to stand.

(2) Players have a right to an interval at half-time.

LAW VIII
The Start of Play

(a) *At the beginning of the game*, choice of ends and the kick-off shall be decided by the toss of a coin. The team winning the toss shall have the option of choice of ends or the kick-off. The Referee having given a signal, the game shall be started by a player taking a place-kick (i.e. a kick at the ball while it is stationary on the ground in the centre of the field of play) into his opponents' half of the field of play. Every player shall be in his own half of the field and every player of the opposing team of the kicker shall remain not less than 10 yards from the ball until it is kicked-off; it shall not be deemed in play until it has travelled the distance of its own circumference. The kicker shall not play the ball a second time until it has been touched or played by another player.

(b) *After a goal is scored*, the game shall be restarted in like manner by a player of the team losing the goal.

(c) *After half-time:* when restarting after half-time, ends shall be changed and the kick-off shall be taken by a player of the opposite team to that of the player who started the game.

Punishment

For any infringement of this Law, the kick-off shall be retaken, except in the case of the kicker playing the ball again before it has been touched or played by another player; for this offence, an indirect free-kick shall be taken by a player of the opposing team from the place where the infringement occurred, subject to the over-riding conditions imposed in Law XIII. A goal shall not be scored direct from a kick-off.

(d) *After any other temporary suspension:* when restarting the game after a temporary suspension of play from any cause not mentioned elsewhere in these Laws, provided that immediately prior to the suspension the ball has not passed over the touch- or goal-lines, the Referee shall drop the ball at the place where it was when play was suspended, unless it was within the goal-area at that time, in which case it shall be dropped on that part of the goal-area line which runs parallel to the goal-line, at the point nearest to where the ball was when play was stopped. It shall be deemed in play when it has touched the ground; if, however, it goes over the touch- or goal-lines after it has been dropped by the Referee, but before it is touched by a player, the Referee shall again drop it. A player shall not play the ball until it has touched the ground. If this section of the Law is not complied with, the Referee shall again drop the ball.

Decisions of the International Board

(1) If, when the Referee drops the ball, a player infringes any of the Laws before the ball has touched the ground, the player concerned shall be cautioned or sent off the field according to the seriousness of the offence, but a free-kick cannot be awarded to the opposing team because the ball was not in play at the time of the offence. The ball shall therefore be again dropped by the Referee.

(2) Kicking-off by persons other than the players competing in a match is prohibited.

LAW IX
Ball In And Out Of Play

The ball is out of play:

(a) When it has wholly crossed the goal-line or touch-line, whether on the ground or in the air.

(b) When the game has been stopped by the Referee.

The ball is in play at all other times from the start of the match to the finish including:

(a) If it rebounds from a goal-post, crossbar or corner flag-post into the field of play.

(b) If it rebounds off either the Referee or Linesmen when they are in the field of play.

(c) In the event of a supposed infringement of the Laws, until a decision is given.

Decisions of the International Board

(1) The lines belong to the areas of which they are the boundaries. In consequence, the touch-lines and the goal-lines belong to the field of play.

LAW X
Method of Scoring

Except as otherwise provided by these

Laws, a goal is scored when the whole of the ball has passed over the goal-line, between the goal-posts and under the crossbar, provided it has not been thrown, carried or intentionally propelled by hand or arm, by a player of the attacking side, except in the case of a goalkeeper who is within his own penalty-area.

The team scoring the greater number of goals during a game shall be the winner; if no goals, or an equal number of goals are scored, the game shall be termed a 'draw'.

Decisions of the International Board

(1) Law X defines the only method according to which a match is won or drawn; no variation whatsoever can be authorised.

(2) A goal cannot in any case be allowed if the ball has been prevented by some outside agent from passing over the goal-line. If this happens in the normal course of play, other than at the taking of a penalty-kick, the game must be stopped and restarted where the ball came into contact with the interference, unless it was within the goal-area at that time, in which case it shall be dropped on that part of the goal-area line which runs parallel to the goal-line, at the point nearest to where the ball was when play was stopped.

(3) If, when the ball is going into goal, a spectator enters the field before it passes wholly over the goal-line, and tries to prevent a score, a goal shall be allowed if the ball goes into goal unless the spectator has made contact with the ball or has interfered with play, in which case the Referee shall stop the game and restart it by dropping the ball at the place where the contact or interference occurred.

LAW XI
Off-Side

(1) A player is in an off-side position if he is nearer to his opponents' goal-line than the ball, unless

a) he is in his own half of the field of play, or

b) there are at least two of his opponents nearer their own goal-line than he is.

(2) A player shall only be declared off-side and penalised for being in an off-side position, if, at the moment the ball touches, or is played by, one of his team, he is, in the opinion of the Referee

a) interfering with play or with an opponent, or

b) seeking to gain an advantage by being in that position.

(3) A player shall not be declared off-side by the Referee

a) merely because of his being in an off-side position, or

b) if he receives the ball, direct, from a goal-kick, a corner-kick, a throw-in, or when it has been dropped by the Referee.

(4) If a player is declared off-side, the Referee shall award an indirect free-kick, which shall be taken by a player of the opposing team from the place where the infringement occurred, unless the offence is committed by a player in his opponents' goal-area, in which case, the free-kick shall be taken from a point anywhere within that half of the goal-area in which the offence occurred.

Decisions of the International Board

(1) Off-side shall not be judged at the

moment the player in question receives the ball, but at the moment when the ball is passed to him by one of his own side. A player who is not in an off-side position when one of his colleagues passes the ball to him or takes a free-kick, does not therefore become off-side if he goes forward during the flight of the ball.

LAW XII

Fouls and Misconduct

A player who intentionally commits any of the following nine offences:
(a) kicks or attempts to kick an opponent;
(b) trips an opponent, i.e. throwing or attempting to throw him by the use of the legs or by stooping in front of or behind him;
(c) jumps at an opponent;
(d) charges an opponent in a violent or dangerous manner;
(e) charges an opponent from behind unless the latter be obstructing;
(f) strikes or attempts to strike an opponent;
(g) holds an opponent;
(h) pushes an opponent;
(i) handles the ball, i.e. carries, strikes or propels the ball with his hand or arm. (This does not apply to the goalkeeper within his own penalty-area.)
shall be penalised by the award of a direct free-kick to be taken by the opposing side from the place where the offence occurred, unless the offence is committed by a player in his opponents' goal-area, in which case, the free-kick shall be taken from a point anywhere within that half of the goal-area in which the offence occurred.

Should a player of the defending side intentionally commit one of the above nine offences within the penalty-area he shall be penalised by a penalty-kick.

A penalty-kick can be awarded irrespective of the position of the ball, if in play, at the time an offence within the penalty-area is committed.

A player committing any of the five following offences:

(1) playing in a manner considered by the Referee to be dangerous, e.g., attempting to kick the ball while held by the goalkeeper;

(2) charging fairly, i.e., with the shoulder, when the ball is not within playing distance of the players concerned and they are definitely not trying to play it;

(3) when not playing the ball, intentionally obstructing an opponent, i.e., running between the opponent and the ball, or interposing the body so as to form an obstacle to an opponent;

(4) charging the goalkeeper except when he
  a) is holding the ball;
  b) is obstructing an opponent;
  c) has passed outside his goal-area.

(5) When playing as goalkeeper and within his own penalty-area,
  a) from the moment he takes control of the ball with his hands, he takes more than four steps in any direction whilst holding, bouncing or throwing the ball in the air and catching it again, without releasing it into play, or, having released the ball into play before, during or after the four steps, he touches it again with his hands, before it has been touched or played by another player of the same team outside of the penalty-area, or by a player of the opposing team either inside or outside of the penalty-area, or

  b) indulges in tactics which, in the opinion of the Referee, are designed merely to hold up the game and thus waste time and so give an unfair advantage to his own team.

shall be penalised by the award of an *indirect free-kick* to be taken by the opposing side from the place where the infringement occurred, subject to the over-riding conditions imposed in Law XIII.

A player shall be *cautioned* if:
(j) he enters or re-enters the field of play to join or rejoin his team after the game has commenced, or leaves the field of play during the progress of the game (except through accident) without, in either case, first having received a signal from the Referee showing him that he may do so. If the Referee stops the game to administer the caution the game shall be restarted by an indirect free-kick taken by a player of the opposing team from the place where the ball was when the Referee stopped the game, subject to the over-riding conditions imposed in Law XIII.

If, however, the offending player has committed a more serious offence, he shall be penalised according to that section of the Law he infringed:

(k) he persistently infringes the Laws of the Game;

(l) he shows, by word or action, dissent from any decision given by the Referee;

(m) he is guilty of ungentlemanly conduct.

For any of these last three offences, in addition to the caution, an *indirect free-kick* shall also be awarded to the opposing side from the place where the offence occurred unless a more serious infringement of the Laws of the Game was committed, subject to the over-riding conditions imposed in Law XIII.

A player shall be *sent off* the field of play if, in the opinion of the Referee,

(n) he is guilty of violent conduct or serious foul play;

(o) he uses foul or abusive language;

(p) he persists in misconduct after having received a caution.

If play be stopped by reason of a player being ordered from the field for an offence without a separate breach of the Law having been committed, the game shall be resumed by an *indirect free-kick* awarded to the opposing side from the place where the infringement occurred, subject to the over-riding conditions imposed in Law XIII.

Decisions of the International Board

(1) If the goalkeeper either intentionally strikes an opponent by throwing the ball vigorously at him or pushes him with the ball while holding it, the Referee shall award a penalty-kick, if the offence took place within the penalty-area.

(2) If a player deliberately turns his back to an opponent when he is about to be tackled, he may be charged but not in a dangerous manner.

(3) In case of body-contact in the goal-area between an attacking player and the opposing goalkeeper not in possession of the ball, the Referee, as sole judge of intention, shall stop the game if, in his opinion, the action of the attacking player was intentional, and award an indirect free-kick.

(4) If a player leans on the shoulders of another player of his own team in order to head the ball, the Referee shall stop the game, caution the player for ungentlemanly conduct and award an indirect free-kick to the opposing side.

(5) A player's obligation when joining or rejoining his team after the start of the match to 'report to the Referee' must be interpreted as meaning 'to draw the attention

203

of the Referee from the touch-line'. The signal from the Referee shall be made by a definite gesture which makes the player understand that he may come into the field of play; it is not necessary for the Referee to wait until the game is stopped (this does not apply in respect of an infringement of Law IV), but the Referee is the sole judge of the moment in which he gives his signal of acknowledgement.

(6) The letter and spirit of Law XII do not oblige the Referee to stop the game to administer a caution. He may, if he chooses, apply the advantage. If he does apply the advantage, he shall caution the player when play stops.

(7) If a player covers up the ball without touching it in an endeavour not to have it played by an opponent, he obstructs but does not infringe Law XII, paragraph 3, because he is already in possession of the ball and covers it for tactical reasons whilst the ball remains within playing distance. In fact, he is actually playing the ball and does not commit an infringement; in this case, the player may be charged because he is in fact playing the ball.

(8) If a player intentionally stretches his arms to obstruct an opponent and steps from one side to the other, moving his arms up and down to delay his opponent, forcing him to change course, but does not make 'bodily contact', the Referee shall caution the player for ungentlemanly conduct and award an indirect free-kick.

(9) If a player intentionally obstructs the opposing goalkeeper, in an attempt to prevent him from putting the ball into play in accordance with Law XII, paragraph 5(a), the Referee shall award an indirect free-kick.

(10) If, after a Referee has awarded a free-kick, a player protests violently by using abusive or foul language and is sent off the field, the free-kick should not be taken until the player has left the field.

(11) Any player, whether he is within or outside the field of play, whose conduct is ungentlemanly or violent, whether or not it is directed towards an opponent, a colleague, the Referee, a Linesman or other person, or who uses foul or abusive language, is guilty of an offence, and shall be dealt with according to the nature of the offence committed.

(12) If, in the opinion of the Referee, a goalkeeper intentionally lies on the ball longer than is necessary, he shall be penalised for ungentlemanly conduct and
   (a) be cautioned and an indirect free-kick awarded to the opposing team;
   (b) in case of repetition of the offence, be sent off the field.

(13) The offence of spitting at opponents, officials or other persons, or similar unseemly behaviour shall be considered as violent conduct within the meaning of section (n) of Law XII.

(14) If, when a Referee is about to caution a player, and before he has done so, the player commits another offence which merits a caution, the player shall be sent off the field of play.

LAW XIII
FREE-KICK

Free-kicks shall be classified under two headings: 'Direct' (from which a goal can be scored direct against the offending side), and 'Indirect' (from which a goal cannot be scored unless the ball has been played or touched by a player other than the kicker before passing through the goal).

When a player is taking a direct or an indirect free-kick inside his own penalty-area, all of the opposing players shall be at least 10 yards from the ball and shall remain outside the penalty-area until the ball has been kicked out of the area. The ball shall be in play immediately it has travelled the distance of its own circumference and is beyond the penalty-area. The goalkeeper shall not receive the ball into his hands, in order that he may thereafter kick it into play. If the ball is not kicked direct into play, beyond the penalty-area, the kick shall be retaken.

When a player is taking a direct or an indirect free-kick outside his own penalty-area, all of the opposing players shall be at least 10 yards from the ball, until it is in play, unless they are standing on their own goal-line, between the goal-posts. The ball shall be in play when it has travelled the distance of its own circumference.

If a player of the opposing side encroaches into the penalty-area, or within 10 yards of the ball, as the case may be, before a free-kick is taken, the Referee shall delay the taking of the kick, until the Law is complied with.

The ball must be stationary when a free-kick is taken, and the kicker shall not play the ball a second time, until it has been touched or played by another player.

Notwithstanding any other reference in these Laws to the point from which a free-kick is to be taken:

(1) Any free-kick awarded to the defending team, within its own goal-area, may be taken from any point within that half of the goal-area in which the free-kick has been awarded.

(2) Any indirect free-kick awarded to the attacking team within its opponents' goal-area shall be taken from that part of the goal-area line which runs parallel to the goal-line, at the point nearest to where the offence was committed.

Punishment

If the kicker, after taking the free-kick, plays the ball a second time before it has been touched or played by another player, an indirect free-kick shall be taken by a player of the opposing team from the spot where the infringement occurred, unless the offence is committed by a player in his opponents' goal-area, in which case the free-kick shall be taken from a point anywhere within that half of the goal-area in which the offence occurred.

Decisions of the International Board

(1) In order to distinguish between a direct and indirect free-kick, the Referee, when he awards an indirect free-kick, shall indicate accordingly by raising an arm above his head. He shall keep his arm in that position until the kick has been taken and retain the signal until the ball has been played or touched by another player or goes out of play.

(2) Players who do not retire to the proper distance when a free-kick is taken must be cautioned and on any repetition be ordered off. It is particularly requested of Referees that attempts to delay the taking of a free-kick by encroaching should be treated as serious misconduct.

(3) If, when a free-kick is being taken, any of the players dance about or gesticulate in a way calculated to distract their opponents, it shall be deemed ungentlemanly conduct for which the offender(s) shall be cautioned.

LAW XIV
PENALTY-KICK

A penalty-kick shall be taken from the penalty-mark and, when it is being taken, all players with the exception of the player taking the kick, properly identified, and the opposing goalkeeper, shall be within the field of play but outside the penalty-area, and at least 10 yards from the penalty-mark. The opposing goalkeeper must stand (without moving his feet) on his own goal-line, between the goal-posts, until the ball is kicked. The player taking the kick must kick the ball forward; he shall not play the ball a second time until it has been touched or played by another player. The ball shall be deemed in play directly it is kicked, i.e., when it has travelled the distance of its circumference. A goal may be scored directly from a penalty-kick. When a penalty-kick is being taken during the normal course of play, or when time has been extended at half-time or full-time to allow a penalty-kick to be taken or retaken, a goal shall not be nullified if, before passing between the posts and under the cross-bar, the ball touches either or both of the goal-posts, or the cross-bar, or the goalkeeper, or any combinations of these agencies, providing that no other infringement has occurred.

Punishment

For any infringement of this Law:

(a) by the defending team, the kick shall be retaken if a goal has not resulted;

(b) by the attacking team other than by the player taking the kick, if a goal is scored it shall be disallowed and the kick retaken.

(c) by the player taking the penalty-kick, committed after the ball is in play, a player of the opposing team shall take an indirect free-kick from the spot where the infringement occurred, subject to the over-riding conditions imposed in Law XIII.

Decisions of the International Board

(1) When the Referee has awarded a penalty-kick, he shall not signal for it to be taken, until the players have taken up position in accordance with the Law.

(2) (a) If, after the kick has been taken, the ball is stopped in its course towards the goal, by an outside agent, the kick shall be retaken.

(b) If, after the kick has been taken, the ball rebounds into play, from the goalkeeper, the crossbar or a goal-post, and is then stopped in its course by an outside agent, the Referee shall stop play and restart it by dropping the ball at the place where it came into contact with the outside agent.

(3) (a) If, after having given the signal for a penalty-kick to be taken, the Referee sees that the goalkeeper is not in his right place on the goal-line, he shall, nevertheless, allow the kick to proceed. It shall be retaken, if a goal is not scored.

(b) If, after the Referee has given the signal for a penalty-kick to be taken, and before the ball has been kicked, the goalkeeper moves his feet, the Referee shall, nevertheless, allow the kick to proceed. It shall be retaken, if a goal is not scored.

(c) If, after the Referee has given the signal for a penalty-kick to be taken, and before the ball is in play, a player of the defending team encroaches into the penalty-area, or within 10 yards of the penalty-mark, the Referee shall, nevertheless, allow the kick to proceed. It shall be retaken, if a goal is not scored.

The player concerned shall be cautioned.

(4) (a) If, when a penalty-kick is being taken, the player taking the kick is guilty of ungentlemanly conduct, the kick, if already taken, shall be retaken, if a goal is scored.

(b) If, after the Referee has given the signal for a penalty-kick to be taken, and before the ball is in play, a colleague of the player taking the kick encroaches into the penalty-area or within 10 yards of the penalty-mark, the Referee shall, nevertheless, allow the kick to proceed. If a goal is scored, it shall be disallowed, and the kick retaken.

(c) If, in the circumstances described in the foregoing paragraph, the ball rebounds into play from the goalkeeper, the crossbar or a goal-post, and a goal has not been scored, the Referee shall stop the game, caution the player and award an indirect free-kick to the opposing team from the place where the infringement occurred, subject to the over-riding conditions imposed in Law XIII.

The colleague of the kicker shall be cautioned.

(5) (a) If, after the referee has given the signal for a penalty-kick to be taken, and before the ball is in play, the goalkeeper moves from his position on the goal-line, or moves his feet, and a colleague of the kicker encroaches into the penalty-area or within 10 yards of the penalty-mark, the kick, if taken, shall be retaken.

The players concerned shall be cautioned.

(b) If, after the Referee has given the signal for a penalty-kick to be taken, and before the ball is in play, a player of each team encroaches into the penalty area, or within 10 yards of the penalty-mark, the kick, if taken, shall be retaken.

(6) When a match is extended, at half-time or full-time, to allow a penalty-kick to be taken or retaken, the extension shall last until the moment that the penalty-kick has been completed, i.e., until the Referee has decided whether or not a goal is scored, and the game shall terminate immediately the Referee has made his decision.

After the player taking the penalty-kick has put the ball into play, no player other than the defending goalkeeper may play or touch the ball before the kick is completed.

(7) When a penalty-kick is being taken in extended time:

(a) the provisions of all the foregoing paragraphs, except paragraphs (2)(b) and (4)(c) shall apply in the usual way, and

(b) in the circumstances described in paragraphs (2)(b) and (4)(c) the game shall terminate immediately the ball rebounds from the goalkeeper, the crossbar or the goal-post.

LAW XV
THROW-IN

When the whole of the ball passes over a touch-line, either on the ground or in the air, it shall be thrown in from the point where it crossed the line, in any direction, by a player of the team opposite to that of the player who last touched it. The thrower at the moment of delivering the ball must face the field of play and part of each foot shall be either on the touch-line or on the ground outside the touch-line. The thrower shall use both hands and shall deliver the ball from behind and over his head. The ball shall be in play immediately it enters the field of play, but the thrower shall not again play the ball until it has been touched or played by another player. A goal shall not be scored direct from a throw-in.

Punishment

(1) If the ball is improperly thrown in, the throw-in shall be taken by a player of the opposing team.

(2) If the thrower plays the ball a second time before it has been touched or played by another player, an indirect free-kick shall be taken by a player of the opposing team from the place where the infringement occurred, subject to the over-riding conditions imposed in Law XIII.

Decisions of the International Board

(1) If a player taking a throw-in, plays the ball a second time by handling it within the field of play before it has been touched or played by another player, the Referee shall award a direct free-kick.

(2) A player taking a throw-in must face the field of play with some part of his body.

(3) If, when a throw-in is being taken, any of the opposing players dance about or gesticulate in a way calculated to distract or impede the thrower, it shall be deemed ungentlemanly conduct for which the offender(s) shall be cautioned.

(4) A throw-in taken from any position other than the point where the ball passed over the touch-line shall be considered to have been improperly thrown in.

LAW XVI
GOAL-KICK

When the whole of the ball passes over the goal-line excluding that portion between the goal-posts, either in the air or on the ground, having last been played by one of the attacking team, it shall be kicked direct into play beyond the penalty-area from a point within that half of the goal-area nearest to where it crossed the line, by a player of the defending team. A goalkeeper shall not receive the ball into his hands from a goal-kick in order that he may thereafter kick it into play. If the ball is not kicked beyond the penalty-area, i.e., direct into play, the kick shall be retaken. The kicker shall not play the ball a second time until it has touched – or been played by – another player. A goal shall not be scored direct from such a kick. Players of the team opposing that of the player taking the goal-kick shall remain outside the penalty-area until the ball has been kicked out of the penalty-area.

Punishment

If a player taking a goal-kick plays the ball a second time after it has passed beyond the penalty-area, but before it has touched or been played by another player, an indirect free-kick shall be awarded to the opposing team, to be taken from the place where the infringement occurred, subject to the over-riding conditions imposed in Law XIII.

Decisions of the International Board

When a goal-kick has been taken and the player who has kicked the ball touches it again before it has left the penalty-area, the kick has not been taken in accordance with the Law and must be retaken.

LAW XVII
CORNER-KICK

When the whole of the ball passes over the goal-line, excluding that portion between the goal-posts, either in the air or on the ground, having last been played by one of the defending team, a member of the attacking team shall take a corner-kick, i.e., the whole of the ball shall be placed within the quarter circle at the nearest corner flag-post, which must not be moved, and it shall be kicked from that position. A goal may be scored direct from such a kick. Players of the team opposing that of the player taking the corner-kick shall not approach within 10 yards of the ball until it is in play, i.e., it has travelled the distance of its own circumference, nor shall the kicker play the ball a second time until it has been touched or played by another player.

Punishment

(1) If the player who takes the kick plays the ball a second time before it has been touched or played by another player, the Referee shall award an indirect free-kick to the opposing team, to be taken from the place where the infringement occurred, subject to the over-riding conditions imposed in Law XIII.

(2) For any other infringement the kick shall be retaken.

Appendix II
The Structure of Football in England

The Football League

First Division   Second Division

Third Division   Fourth Division

GM Vauxhall Conference (winners each
year qualify for entry to the Football League)

Professional, semi-professional and amateur leagues including:

Anglian Combination
Carlisle & District
Central
Central Midlands
Combined Counties
Dorset Combination
Eastern Counties
Essex
Football Combination
Gloucestershire County
Hellenic
Herts County
Kent
Lancashire Amateur
Leicestershire Senior
Lincolnshire
Liverpool Combination
London Spartan
Manchester

Mid-Cheshire
Midland Combination
Northern
Northern Alliance
Northern Counties East
Northern Premier
North West Counties
Notts Alliance
Peterborough & District
Somerset Senior
Southern
Southern Amateur
South Midlands
South Western
Staffordshire Senior
Suffolk & Ipswich
Sussex County
Teesside
United Counties

Vauxhall-Opel
Wearside
Wessex
West Cheshire
Western
West Midlands

Cup competitions

FA Challenge Cup
Littlewoods Cup
Sherpa Van Trophy
Simod Cup
FA Challenge Trophy
FA Challenge Vase
FA Sunday Cup
FA Youth Cup
FA County Youth Cup

Appendix III: Glossary of Football Terms

Anchor man – midfield player whose chief function is to win the ball.

Angle – applied to the direction the ball is travelling. Goal-keepers come off their line to 'narrow the angle'. Forwards will drop off opponents to make a better passing angle for a colleague.

Assist – the player who provides the pass for a goal is credited with 'an assist'.

Ball watching – watching the ball to the exclusion of your opponent.

Blindside – the opposite side of a player to the ball.

Block tackle – tackle made in an upright position, with the side of the foot facing the opponent.

Box – the penalty-area.

Byline – the goal-line.

Channels – term used to describe areas of play on either side of the pitch (*Fig. 130*).

Checking – moving one way and stopping to run off in another direction.

Chip – a pass made by a stabbing action of the kicking foot to achieve a sharp trajectory.

Close down – to deny an opponent space.

Committing a defender – ensuring that an opponent is brought into play by moving towards him.

Conditioned play – a training exercise where a condition is imposed, e.g., all passes must be first time.

Creating space – increasing the distance from opponents.

Cross – to play the ball from a wide position into a more central position.

Fig. 130

Cross over – two attacking players moving in different directions past each other.

Cushion – to control the ball by withdrawing the surface in contact with the ball, e.g., the inside of the foot or the thigh.

The 'D' – the arc marked outside the penalty-area.

Decoy run – a run to take a defender out of position with the aim of creating space for a colleague.

Diagonal run – a run at an angle.

Disguise –	concealing your intentions by pretending to do one thing and then doing something else.	**One touch –**	passing the ball first time, i.e., without controlling it first.
Dribble –	an attacker taking the ball past one or more opponents.	**One-two –**	a quick exchange of passes between two players.
Dummy –	in dribbling, feinting to move in one direction to unbalance an opponent and moving away in the other direction.	**Overlap –**	moving ahead of a colleague in possession of the ball.
		Pressure training –	performing a technique many times in training in a limited period of time.
Far post –	the further post from where the player is standing.	**Push pass –**	pass made with the inside of the kicking foot.
Feint –	a deceptive movement with or without the ball.	**Run with the ball –**	movement with the ball in space.
Flank –	the area of the pitch near the touch-lines.	**Screen –**	to shield the ball to prevent an opponent reaching it.
Flight –	the trajectory of the ball.	**Sell –**	to 'sell' yourself means committing yourself to go for the ball when the odds favour the opponent.
Goalside –	a position between the ball and the goal you are defending.		
		Shadow play –	coaching exercises without the ball.
Half-volley –	contact with the ball as it strikes the ground.	**Show –**	to 'show' means to make yourself available for a pass.
Hold –	to retain possession.		
Hustle –	to put an opponent in possession of the ball under pressure.	**Sliding tackle –**	tackle from the side, along the ground.
		Small-sided games –	practice games in small groups.
Instep –	the upper surface of the foot or boot, i.e., where the laces are.	**Split runs –**	runs made by players in opposite directions in order to create more space.
Jockey –	a defender taking up a position to influence which way an opponent will try to go round him.	**Spread –**	a goalkeeper 'spreads' himself to block the view of goal of an attacking player by use of his arms and body.
Lofted drive –	a powerful kick with the instep through the bottom half of the ball.	**Striker –**	attacker whose main function is to score.
Man-for-man marking –	marking one opponent exclusively.	**Supporting player –**	one who positions himself to receive a pass from the man in possession.
Mark –	to take up a position to deny the opponent the ball or tackle him.	**Sweeper –**	the defender who is spare at the back.
Near post –	the nearer post to where the player is standing.	**Tackle –**	a challenge to win the ball by use of the feet.
Off-side –	see Law XI in Appendix I, Laws of the Game.	**Taking players on –**	dribbling past opponents.

Technique – a single performance of a skill.

Through-ball – a pass through the opposing defence, usually up the middle, for a player to run on to in space.

Trap – to control the ball.

Turning the opponent – forcing an opponent to turn by playing the ball past him.

Turning with the ball – receiving the ball when facing your goal and turning the other way.

Two touch – controlling the ball first, then passing it.

Wall – defensive barrier formed by players to block a free-kick near goal.

Wall pass – using a colleague as a 'wall' to collect a return pass.

Wedge – control of the ball by using the foot as a wedge, i.e., to trap the ball on the ground.

Weight, of the pass – the pace of the ball when passed.

WM formation – a formation of play, widely used in England before 1953, so-called because the positions of players corresponded to the points of these letters.

Volley – contact with the ball while it is in the air.

Index